College Majors and Careers

A Resource Guide for Effective Life Planning

4th Edition

by Paul Phifer

Director, Career Resource Center

Grand Rapids Community College

Copyright © 2000 Paul Phifer
ISBN 0-89434-278-9

Library of Congress Cataloging-in-Publication Data
Phifer, Paul.
    College majors and careers: a resource guide for effective life planning / by
Paul Phifer.—4th ed.
    p. cm.
Includes bibliographical references and indexes.
ISBN 0-89434-278-9
    1. Vocational guidance—United States. 2. Vocational interests—United States.
3. College majors—United States. 4. Professions—United States. I. Title.
HF5382.5.U5P445   2000
331.7'02'0973—dc21   99-37769
                                                CIP

Printed in the United States of America

Cover design by Shock Digital Art

Published and distributed by
Ferguson Publishing Company
200 West Jackson Blvd., 7th Floor
Chicago, IL 60606
312-692-1000
http://www.fergpubco.com

Y-7

About the Author

Paul Phifer has nearly 30 years' experience as an educator at both the high school and college levels. He currently serves as the director of the Career Resource Center at Grand Rapids Community College. Paul holds a master's degree in guidance and counseling from Western Michigan University and is a Certified Career Development Facilitator Curriculum Instructor, a Licensed Professional Counselor (LPC), a National Certified Counselor (NCC), and a National Certified Career Counselor (NCCC). A father of four, Paul Phifer has long been active in his community, first as a Big Brother and now as a Christian Career Development Facilitator for his church.

Acknowledgements

I would like to express my gratitude for the advice and support given to me by the Ferguson Publishing staff. In addition, I am particularly grateful to the Grand Rapids Community College administration for their continuing administrative support of my requests for updated materials, computers, and ongoing professional exposures, which has allowed me to maintain and enrich career development activities for students and nonstudents, both locally and nationally. I am also thankful for the many career writers from whose research and publications I was privileged to draw. Although not mentioned in bibliographical form, their works provided this resource with the degree of accuracy and quality required. But most importantly, I must acknowledge my Savior, Jesus Christ, whose indwelling spirit deserves all the credit for anything I might have included within these pages that may serve to enable the user to live a more directed and fulfilling life.

Dedication

To my wife, Margaret, for her continuing support of whatever I have endeavored to seriously pursue.

Contents

Introduction 1

I. Clusters of Majors 3

II. Who Will Be Helped by This Book? 5

III. How This Book Is Organized and How to Use It 7

IV. Choosing the Major that Best Reflects You 10
    Accounting 11
    Aerospace Engineering 14
    Agriculture 17
    Allied Health Assisting and Technology 20
    Allied Health Sciences 23
    Anthropology 26
    Architecture 29
    Art 32
    Astronomy 35
    Banking and Finance 38
    Biology 41
    Botany 44
    Business Administration and Management 47
    Chemical Engineering 50
    Chemistry 53
    Civil Engineering 56
    Communications 59
    Computer Science 62
    Construction 65
    Culinary Arts 68
    Economics 71
    Education 74
    Electrical/Electronic Engineering .77
    Electrical/Electronics Technology .80
    English 83
    Food and Beverage Management/Service 86
    Foreign Language 89
    Forestry 92
    Geography 95
    Geology 98
    Health Administration, Management, and Related Services . .101
    History 104
    Home Economics 107
    Horticulture 110

Hotel/Motel Management 113
Industrial Engineering 116
Industrial and Precision Production/Technology 119
Law 122
Legal and Protective Services 125
Library and Information Sciences 128
Marketing and Distribution 131
Mathematics 134
Mechanical Engineering 137
Mechanics and Related Services 140
Medicine 143
Metallurgical and Mining Engineering 146
Military Science 149
Nursing and Related Services 152
Performing Arts 155
Philosophy 158
Physics 161
Physiology 164
Political Science 167
Psychology 170
Recreation and Leisure 173
Religion and Theology 176
Secretarial Science 179
Social Work 182
Sociology 185
Transportation 188
Zoology 191

V. Career-Related Questions and Answers
1 What does the word *career* mean? 194
2 What is career decision-making? 194
3 Is career development different for an older adult than for a
younger person? 194
4 What is career success? 195
5 What is a career resource or information center? 195
6 Are career development and placement services the same? . 195
7 What are career development services? 196
8 What are job placement services? 196
9 What does a good career counselor do? 196
10 What is a self-assessment? 197
11 What is a college major? 197
12 What should I know before selecting a major? 197
13 How do I actually select a major? 198

14 What should I do if I want a college degree but don't know what to pick for my major? 199

15 What should I do if I only want to pursue a short-term program of a year or less? 200

16 I must register for a full load of classes tomorrow but don't know what to take—what should I do? 200

17 What is an MBA? 200

18 Should I go for an MBA? 201

19 Should I get a Ph.D.? 202

20 What is an apprenticeship? 203

21 What is co-op education? 204

22 What are home study courses? 204

23 What is virtual education? 205

24 What is an internship? 205

25 What is mentoring? 206

26 What is networking and can it help me? 207

27 What are "high-tech" jobs? 207

28 How do I know if a program or institution is good? 207

29 What is a liberal arts major? 208

30 What are career tests? 209

31 Should the results of my career tests determine what I do in the future? 209

32 Should I accept career test results that point to a single field? .209

33 What does it mean when the results of my career testing show that I am interested in just about everything? 210

34 Am I required to take a battery of tests to effectively plan my career? 210

35 What is the difference between an aptitude test and an interest inventory? 211

36 Should I "test out" of a required course? 212

37 Can occupational projections be trusted? 213

38 What are some common problems that often hamper career development? 213

Appendices
    A. Descriptions of Selected Occupations 215
    B. Definitions of Selected Skill Statements 243
    C. Definitions of Values and Personal Attributes 245

Index of Occupations 248

Introduction

College Majors and Careers is designed to help students and prospective students of all ages with the critical decision of choosing a focus in a collegiate program. Whether you are just graduating from high school and preparing to enter a four-year college or planning a midlife career change, this book can help.

You will find descriptions of more than 60 college majors along with a list of careers each major commonly leads to, skills and personality traits best suited for those careers, degree requirements, ways to enhance your knowledge and skills outside the classroom, and resources for more information.

Why is there a need for a guide of this type? To answer this question requires a closer look at the society in which we live. It is a society that is changing at a phenomenal pace. In the last 30 years, computerization has transformed the United States from a primarily industrial nation to one with an overwhelming emphasis on information and services.

Such changes have brought unprecedented comforts, conveniences, and leisure time—but they also have created a more complex and stressful lifestyle for many Americans. The cost of living has skyrocketed; new concerns have arisen about crime, the quality of education, and the condition of our environment; and family structures have changed dramatically.

The job security enjoyed by previous generations is becoming a fading memory as companies downsize and make other short-term economic decisions in an increasingly competitive and global marketplace. The hiring of temporary workers and outsourcing have become routine, and job turnover rates are high.

These factors, combined with the unfulfilled personal needs experienced by many, are spurring increasing numbers of people to return to school or change careers. As a result, the business of career planning services is booming.

In this environment, it is more important than ever to start early in determining a career path. This means not only choosing the college major that is right for you, but also recognizing that an occupation alone will not lead to a fulfilling life. In your educational pursuits, it is important to consider life's other major aspects: family, religion, and leisure activities. Today's society demands a comprehensive sense of direction, including a healthy balance of professional and personal activity.

This does not mean that you should make a mad rush to select the right curriculum or job. What it does mean is that you should become thoughtfully involved in the process of determining the educational, occupational, and leisure-time activities that most strongly support your basic values and bring the deepest meaning and purpose to your life. This is a lifelong process, and when approached correctly, it will reflect your unique personality configuration and lead to true fulfillment.

But the process of choosing a college major can be daunting. *College Majors and Careers* aims to motivate students to begin a realistic assessment of their lives and career goals. Its special mission is to help students who are saturated with information or experiencing apprehension from a lack of career awareness or direction. By linking the selection of a college major—and associated occupations—with your personality traits and preferences, the book should help you to narrow your focus and choose an academic and occupational direction that is likely to be most fulfilling for you.

Keep in mind that this book is intended as a starting point only. Human beings are complex, and each individual has his or her own personality, needs, talents, and goals. Further research and a consultation with a career counselor is highly recommended. Additional career information can be found in career resource centers, counseling offices, libraries, and departmental offices.

Good luck on your journey!

Section I
Clusters of Majors

The majors are presented alphabetically, but each one may be viewed as a member of a family of related majors. History and political science, for example, are both in the social science field.

Here's how the majors cluster in general fields:

Agriculture and Horticulture
Agriculture
Forestry
Horticulture

Architecture, Construction, and Technology
Architecture
Construction
Electrical/Electronics Technology
Industrial and Precision Technology
Mechanics and Related Services
Transportation

Business and Related Areas
Accounting
Banking and Finance
Business Administration and Management
Hotel/Motel Management
Marketing and Distribution
Secretarial Science

Culinary Arts, Food Service, and Recreation
Culinary Arts
Food and Beverage Management/Service
Home Economics
Recreation and Leisure

Engineering
Aerospace
Chemical
Civil
Electrical/Electronic
Industrial
Mechanical
Metallurgical and Mining

Fine and Performing Arts
Art
Performing Arts

Government, Public Service, and Related Areas
Education
Law
Legal and Protective Services
Library and Information Sciences
Military Science
Religion and Theology
Social Work

Health Care, Medicine, and Nursing
Allied Health Assisting and Technology
Allied Health Sciences
Health Administration, Management, and Related Services
Medicine
Nursing and Related Services

Language Arts
Communications
English
Foreign Language
Philosophy

Life Sciences
Biology
Botany
Physiology
Zoology

Physical Sciences and Math
Astronomy
Chemistry
Computer Science
Geology
Mathematics
Physics

Social Sciences
Anthropology
Economics
Geography
History
Political Science
Psychology
Sociology

Section II

Who Will Be Helped by This Book?

College Majors and Careers is a valuable reference guide for...

Students

- Introduces them to a wide variety of college courses, giving them an overview of their content and how they relate to other fields of study.
- Emphasizes personal traits associated with success in each major and in careers that most logically follow that major.
- Lists leisure activities associated with various majors.
- Gives the approximate length and level of education required for employment in related occupations.
- Provides a sampling of preparatory high school courses for each major.
- Offers answers to many career-related questions and answers.
- Provides a summary description of each major field.
- Lists transferable skills useful in pursuing various academic programs.
- Serves as a springboard and motivation for more in-depth and focused career exploration.
- Cites resources and organizations providing more information about each field.

Junior and Senior High School Counselors

- Augments existing data on college study and occupational life.
- Helps motivate students by clearly showing the relationships between study and later life.
- Serves as a resource for teacher inservice and counselor training sessions.
- Provides valuable information for assisting students with college major planning, helping to reduce curriculum, program, and course misplacement.
- Lists organizations and books for more background information.
- Offers a sampling of preparatory courses to help students plan an appropriate four-year program.
- Provides answers to career-related questions asked by many students as well as responses to concerns of students with special needs.

Parents

- Helps to clearly define the relationship between college study and work.
- Provides background for discussing college plans with children who are current or prospective college students.
- Cites references and resources for additional exploration.

Teachers

- Highlights the importance of career guidance. Makes it easier to motivate students by citing jobs related to their studies. Provides information useful in course orientation and introductions.
- Provides information to help suggest career options to students.
- Stimulates more self-exploration on the part of students.
- Encourages use of the classroom as a laboratory for career exploration activities.
- Provides information which may help misplaced or misguided students.
- Encourages high school and college academic departments to become more aware and sensitive to the career activities of their graduates.
- Provides a textbook for use in career education classes or as a referral source in libraries.
- Provides answers to many questions frequently asked by students.

College Counselors and Other Student Personnel Workers

- Offers valuable help in counseling, attracting, and recruiting students in the admissions process.
- Provides background for building closer links between the counseling staff and academic departments.
- Provides a base of knowledge useful in meeting student questions about educational programs and career options.
- Answers many questions frequently asked by students, including those with special needs.
- Suggests part-time and summer job options that may be closely related to students' academic training and potential career choices.
- Serves as a useful reference resource to be used by counseling center clients as a part of their self-development research.
- Shows employers how various aspects of college support services help educate and prepare future employees.
- Provides information related to career direction suitability that should be useful for Upward Bound and Special Services personnel in meeting governmental guidelines.

How This Book Is Organized and How to Use It

Each of the college majors and career briefs featured contains information presented in a consistent format for easy reference. Each entry begins with a general definition of the major field then continues with the sections described below.

High School Courses

Lists high school courses or areas which are closely related to the major or considered useful background for that field. Course titles vary greatly among high schools as well as grade levels. Courses cited are not all-inclusive and are intended to be used as a general guideline by students, parents, teachers, and counselors. Educators will need to exercise professional expertise and include local courses that may apply to a particular field but are not listed. It is strongly suggested that students consult with counselors concerning preparatory courses related to particular fields of study.

Related Occupations

Lists jobs appropriate for graduates with that major, followed by the average minimum level of education required. Some occupations listed in this section require additional, specialized academic training for licensure and/or full professional status. Interested students are encouraged to contact a career counselor or academic advisor about these requirements before making a decision.

Following is a key for the codes used in this section:

AA = Associate degree (or two full years of college study after high school) generally required or very helpful. In some cases, people enter the field after taking specialized courses that may not require two full years.

B = Bachelor's degree (or four full years of college study after high school) generally required or helpful. This may be a BA (Bachelor of Arts) or BS (Bachelor of Science) degree.

C = Certificate, normally awarded following successful completion of one year or less of training and/or formal college education.

M = Master's degree preferred for the field; usually requires one or two years of study after the bachelor's. This may be an MA (Master of Arts) or MS (Master of Science) degree.

P = First professional degree required; usually after completion of bachelor's degree. Some professional degrees include the BD (Bachelor of Divinity); LLB (law school degree); MD (Doctor of Medicine) and DDS (Doctor of Dental Science).

D = Doctoral degree, preferred for full professional status in the field. These include the Ph.D. and Ed.D., which usually take from three to five years after the bachelor's degree. However, interested students often enter this field as a Research Assistant (RA) or Administrative Assistant (AA).

V = Indicates requirements vary greatly and/or vocational training is generally required; may include a combination of academic and work experience.

Sometimes, two or more codes appear after an occupation, which means that employers may hire candidates with different levels of education for the same job. For example, under Communications, employers might hire a news photographer with either a two-year certificate or a four-year bachelor's degree, depending on the candidate's other characteristics and qualifications. Definitions for the least familiar of the cited occupations appear in Appendix A.

Leisure Activities

Identifies hobbies, interests, and activities related to the major as well as to many of the occupations cited. This list provides a clearer picture of how extracurricular activities are related to majors, occupations, and other life endeavors.

Skills

Presents a partial list of skills that may be related to success in the major or related occupations or are frequently used in either. Some are natural inborn traits (aptitudes); others are acquired through practice, study, or extra effort (abilities). Some of the skills may be developed or discovered while the person is advancing in a course of study or occupation. The list of skills also provides a valuable and time-saving stop-check for students who may be mistakenly moving in an unsuitable direction. Definitions of skill statements that may be unfamiliar or difficult to understand can be found in Appendix B.

Values and Attributes

Lists some of the motivations and personal characteristics generally associated with the field of study. This is not to imply that other values are not present or that these values are held by everyone interested in the subject. The values listed should help students to determine if the subject, and those related to it, will move them closer to what is really most important to them in life. Definitions of some of the values and attributes that may be unfamiliar or hard to interpret can be found in Appendix C.

Resources

Lists books and/or professional associations that can provide additional information related to the major. For names of other associations in the major field of interest, see the *Encyclopedia of Associations* (published by Gale Research Company) or *National Trade and Professional Associations of the United States* (published annually by Columbia Books). These should be available in the reference section of most public libraries. Readers should augment the resources cited in this book with references recommended by a local counselor or teacher. Obviously, some of the references cited are subject to change due to books going out of print, revisions and updates, address changes, etc.

Please be aware that due to similarities in definition, the words major, college majors, fields of study, fields, subject, and like terms are used interchangeably and all refer to one's major area of study.

Career-Related Questions and Answers

After all of the entries on college majors, this section provides answers to "key" career-related questions either frequently asked by students or considered to be important for certain populations. As a career counselor, I have been asked the same or similar questions dozens of times by students, parents, and other professionals over the years—these are the most common questions along with their answers.

Choosing the Major that Best Reflects You

This section describes and offers pertinent information about more than 60 of the most popular college majors today.

Most users will be able to acquire valuable insight by simply browsing through and identifying those majors that most interest them. However, it is suggested that you use this popular approach as a stop-check measurement only. To obtain the maximum benefit, you should locate and complete a self-assessment. Doing a self-assessment consists of identifying and then summarizing your most pronounced personality attributes and most cherished life and work values. Finally, while some can effectively conduct such an assessment on their own, it is strongly recommended that you consult a qualified career counselor to confirm your initial findings.

Accounting

Accounting involves the examination, organization, management, and design of accurate recording and reporting procedures of financial and business transactions. The study of accounting helps students learn the various ways of maintaining accurate, up-to-date financial and business records. This includes a focus on methods of compilation, verification supervision, revision, examination, efficiency recording, designing, and reporting of such practices for both individuals and businesses. Knowledge and implementation of good accounting procedures are required if financial or business success is to be realized, whether it be for an individual, family, or business. Major specializations include public accounting, management accounting, tax accounting, cost accounting, government accounting, budget accounting, and internal auditing.

High School Courses

Business	Math
Business Math	Consumer Math
Accounting	Bookkeeping
Computer Operations	Computer Programming
Banking	Economics
Statistics	

Related Occupations

Accountant—-B	Actuary—-B
Auditor—-B	Bank Officer—-AA/B
Bookkeeper—-V/AA	Budget Accountant—-B
Computer Systems Analyst—-B	Controller—-B/M
Cost Accountant—-B	Credit Manager—-AA/B
Economist—-B	Educator—-B/D
Financial Analyst—-B	Financial Planner—-B
Insurance Agent—-V/B	Internal Auditor—-B
Internal Revenue Agent—-B	International Accountant—-B
Investment Banker—-B	Management Accountant—-B
Management Consultant—-B/M	Market Research Analyst—-B
Programmer—-B	Public Accountant—-B
Purchasing Agent—-B	Statistician—-B
Tax Accountant—-AA/B	Tax Preparer—-V/B
Treasurer—-B	Underwriter—-B

Leisure Activities

Working as a part-time or volunteer treasurer or income tax preparer; maintaining an accurate personal checkbook; joining a professional accounting organization; reading accounting-related publications; joining a financial advisory board; solving problems involving analytical and logical processes; attending accounting-related lectures, trade shows or conventions; working as a student aide in a high school or college accounting department; working with a personal computer.

Skills

- Proficiency in written and oral communication
- Ability to organize, analyze, and interpret numerical data
- Aptitude for accuracy and detail
- Proficiency with computers
- Ability to work alone and concentrate for long periods of time
- Ability to make sound judgments and decisions and to solve quantitative problems
- Ability to explain complex financial data to others
- Intellectual capacity to do well in most undergraduate and graduate college programs
- Ability to lead, supervise, and direct others

Values and Attributes

- Achievement
- Tendency toward analytical and logical thinking
- Patience
- Intellectual growth
- Integrity
- Independence
- Capacity for precision, detail, and order
- Thoroughness
- Recognition and appreciation from others
- Alertness
- Ability to frame inquiry and respond objectively
- Resourcefulness
- Skill with numbers
- Imagination

Resources

- Gaylord, Gloria and Glenda Reid. *Careers in Accounting: Third Edition.* VGM Career Horizons, 1998.
- Goldberg, Jan. *Great Jobs for Accounting Majors.* VGM Career Horizons, 1998.
- **American Institute of Certified Public Accountants**
  1211 Avenue of the Americas
  New York, NY 10036
  212-596-6200
  http://aicpa.org/
  (publishes preparation information for CPA examinations)
- **American Society of Women Accountants**
  60 Revere Drive, Suite 500
  Northbrook, IL 60062
  800-326-2163
  http://www.aswa.org/
  (offers scholarships and promotes interests of women in accounting)

Aerospace Engineering

Aerospace engineering is the study of the practical application of physical science and mathematics in the research, design, development, testing, launching, and production of aircraft, spacecraft, navigational systems, and related equipment, systems, and processes in an efficient and economical manner. It involves the design and production of power units, vehicle structure, aerodynamics and guidance control as well as airplane, rocket, missile, and satellite launching. Specialties include aircraft design, guidance systems, instrumentation, fluid mechanics, thermodynamics, satellites, helicopters, rockets, and military aircraft.

High School Courses

Math	Algebra
Geometry	Trigonometry
Calculus	Drawing
Mechanical Drawing	Computers
Computer Science	Physical Science
Chemistry	Physics
Mechanics	

Related Occupations

Aerodynamist—-B	Aeronautical Engineer—-B/D
Aerospace Airplane Pilot—-AA/B	Aerospace Engineer—-B/D
Astronomer—-D	Astrophysicist—-B/D
Computer Programmer—-B	Computer Science Engineer—-B
Consulting Engineer—-B/D	Electrical Engineer—-B
Environmental Engineer—-B	Marine Engineer—-B
Mechanical Engineer—-B	Metallurgical Engineer—-B
Nuclear Engineer—-B/D	Petroleum Engineer—-B
Physicist—-B/D	Research Engineer—-B
Safety Engineer—-B	Systems Analyst—-B
Systems Engineer—-B	

Leisure Activities

Reading publications related to flying or space; viewing aircraft or space-related documentaries and programs on TV or at the movies; browsing the Internet for aviation-related topics; developing hobbies or collections related to model airplanes, cars, mechanics, or electronic games and equipment; air travel; attending lectures or conferences related to aviation or engineering; visiting science museums and exhibits; belonging to a club or organization such as the American Institute of Aeronautics and Astronautics; solving analytic and logic problems.

Skills

- High proficiency in mathematics and physical sciences
- Ability to analyze, organize, and interpret scientific data
- Ability to work well with others
- Ability to make keen observations and sound judgments
- Aptitude for accuracy and detail, spatial perception and abstract reasoning
- Sensitivity to economic considerations and human needs
- Proficiency in an area of specialization and of current practices and trends
- Ability to conduct and clearly communicate results of scientific research
- Intellectual capacity to perform well in most undergraduate and graduate college programs
- Proficiency with computers

Values and Attributes

- Creativity
- Knowledge
- Achievement
- Desire to help others live better
- Strong interest in aviation and space
- Interest in seeing ideas developed into practical use
- Curiosity
- Imagination
- Perseverance
- Responsibility
- Capability
- Integrity

Resources

- **American Institute of Aeronautics and Astronautics**
  1801 Alexander Bell Drive, Suite 500
  Reston, VA 20191
  703-264-7500
  (offers job placement service, publishes *AIAA Student Journal,* and provides
  career information)
- **Society of Women Engineers**
  20 Wall Street, 11th Floor
  New York, NY 10005-3902
  212-509-0224
  http://www.swe.org
  (offers scholarships, job placement service, provides information on achievements
  of women in engineering, conducts surveys, and publishes career guidance
  pamphlets)

Agriculture

Agriculture is the science of growing crops and raising livestock. It involves planting, cultivating, fertilizing, harvesting, processing, and distributing fruits, vegetables, and nursery stock. It also includes the raising, feeding, breeding, and marketing of livestock. In addition, agricultural study exposes the student to the various by-products of livestock such as dairy products, eggs, honey, and fur. Agricultural research related to increasing the yield and quality of products and by-products, sanitation, diseases, methods of efficiency, and other areas is another important part of the field.

High School Courses

Math	Algebra
Geometry	Trigonometry
Food Science	Earth Science
Biology	Chemistry
Landscape Gardening	Zoology

Related Occupations

Agricultural Engineer—-B	Agronomist—-B/D
Animal Scientist—-B/D	Biochemist—-B/D
Biologist—-B/D	Botanist—-B/D
Cattle Farmer—-B/V	Chemical Lab Technician—-AA
Cooperative Extension Agent—-B	Dairy Farmer—-B/V
Educator—-B/D	Entomologist—-B/D
Farm Equipment Mechanic—-AA/V	Farmer—-B/V
Feed Store Operator—-V	Fish Farmer—-B/V
Florist—-V	Food Scientist—-B
Horticulturist—-B/D	Laboratory Assistant—-AA
Landscape Gardener—-AA	Microbiologist—-B/D
Nursery Manager—-V	Parasitologist—-B/D
Physiologist—-D	Soil Conservationist—-B/D
Soil Physicists—-B/D	Veterinarian—-P

Leisure Activities

Working part-time or as a volunteer on a farm, ranch, pet shop, garden center, or zoo; gardening; owning and caring for pets; belonging to Future Farmers of America or 4-H; scouting; attending farm shows and fairs; working as a student aide or volunteer in a school science or college agriculture department; attending clinics, lectures, and workshops related to agriculture; reading agriculture-related publications; developing hobbies and collections related to gardening, horses, or raising livestock.

Skills

- Good understanding of and familiarity with agricultural techniques and applications
- Physical stamina, good vision, and manual dexterity
- Ability to recognize differences in shapes, shading, and color
- Proficiency in reading and writing
- Ability to make keen observations and sound judgments
- Ability to organize, analyze, and interpret scientific data
- Ability to make appropriate decisions and apply scientific methods to agricultural concerns
- Ability to manage and supervise others
- Able to work both alone as well as with others
- General knowledge of farm supplies, equipment, services, and business/marketing practices
- Aptitude for science and mathematics

Values and Attributes

- Independence
- Desire to help people
- Achievement
- Strong interest in agriculture
- Fondness for outdoor activities
- Ability to adapt to frequent changes
- Patience
- Responsibility
- Perseverance
- Resourcefulness
- Industriousness

Resources

- **National FFA Organization**
  6060 FFA Drive
  PO Box 68960
  Indianapolis, IN 46268
  317-802-6060
  http://www.ffa.org
  (supplements training programs for agricultural careers, offers career planning and scholarships)

Allied Health Assisting and Technology

Allied health assisting and technology involves the study of areas of technological support and health-related assistance to physicians, dentists, and other health professionals. The skills and services learned in this field of study are considered essential to effective health care services. Among the various specializations are dental assisting, hygiene, and technology; medical laboratory technology and assisting; radiography; health care; dietetics and nutrition; and physical and occupational therapy.

High School Courses

Science	Biology
Health	First Aid

Related Occupations

Biomedical Equipment Technician—-AA

Cytotechnologist—-AA/B	Dental Assistant—-AA
Dental Hygienist—-AA	Dental Lab Technician—-AA

Diagnostic Medical Sonographer—-AA

Dietetic Technician—-AA	EEG Technologist—-AA
EKG Technician—-AA	Emergency Medical Technician—-AA

Environmental Health Technician—-AA

Medical Assistant—-AA	Medical Lab Technician—-AA
Medical Records Technician—-AA	Mental Health Technician—-AA

Occupational Therapy Assistant—-AA

Operating Room Technician—-AA	Ophthalmic Medical Assistant—-AA
Optician—-AA	Optometric Assistant—-AA
Perfusionist—-V	Physical Therapy Assistant—-AA
Physician Assistant—-AA/B	Podiatric Assistant—-AA

Prosthetic and Orthotic Technician—-AA

Radiological Technologist—-AA	Respiratory Therapy Technician—-AA
Surgical Technician—-AA	Veterinary Technician—-AA
X-Ray Technician—-AA	

Leisure Activities

Attending science fairs; visiting museums and exhibits; reading health-related publications; serving as an aide in a church or health agency; working part-time in a hospital, medical center, or nursing home; attending lectures and workshops related to health care services; watching health-related movies or TV dramas; actively supporting health care expansion and medical research drives.

Skills

- Ability to react quickly and maintain emotional and physical composure in stressful situations
- High proficiency for accuracy and detail
- Proficiency in interpersonal communication
- Proficiency in memorization and giving and receiving directions
- Physical stamina, good vision, and manual dexterity
- Ability to make keen observations, sound judgments, and appropriate decisions
- Ability to work cooperatively with people of differing backgrounds and responsibilities
- Good motor coordination

Values and Attributes

- Achievement
- Desire to help others
- Health
- Wisdom
- Interest in challenges and working directly with people
- Helpful and friendly attitude
- Sensitivity to the needs and pain of others
- Willingness to work irregular hours and on weekends
- Industriousness
- Capability
- Poise
- Dependability
- Resourcefulness

Resources

- *Exploring Health Care Careers: Real People Tell You What You Need to Know.* Ferguson Publishing Company, 1998.
- Metcalf, Zubie, Ed.D. *Career Planning Guide for the Allied Health Professions.* Williams & Wilkins, 1998.
- **American Medical Technologists Association**
  710 Higgins Road
  Park Ridge, IL 60068
  Tel. 847-823-5169
  http://www.amtl.com/
  (offers information about certification exams for lab assistants, phlebotomists, and dental assistants)
- **American Society of Radiologic Technologists**
  15000 Central Avenue SE
  Albuquerque, NM 87123
  800-444-2778
  http://www.asrt.org/
  (offers student scholarships and job placement services)

Allied Health Sciences

Allied health sciences is the study of health science areas that are related to and supportive of medical services provided by physicians and dentists. Students are exposed to ways of supporting and maintaining health care and medical services for individuals and populations. In addition, students learn about scientific educational and social approaches to prevention and control of disease, sickness, and injury. Special areas of concentration include environmental health, occupational safety and health, dental and medical technology, research, and health education.

High School Courses

Science	Biology
Physiology	Chemistry
Health	Algebra
Geometry	Trigonometry

Related Occupations

Biomedical Engineer—-B	Biostatistician—-B/M
Blood Bank Specialist—-B	Clinical Chemist—-B
Dental Hygienist—-AA/B	Dietician—-B
Health Educator—-B/D	Health Microbiologist—-B
Hospital Administrator—-M	Medical Engineer—-B
Medical Illustrator—-B	Medical Technologist—-B
Nuclear Medical Technologist—-B	Nutritionist—-B
Pharmacist—-B	Physician Assistant—-AA/B
Prosthetic Orthotist—-AA/B	Radiation Therapy Technologist—-AA
Radiologic Health Specialist—-B	Technical Writer—-B
Tissue Technologist—-V	

Leisure Activities

Attending science fairs, health exhibits, and visiting museums; reading health science-related publications; doing lab experiments and researching health science-related topics; working part-time or as a volunteer for a health agency, hospital, or school health science department; writing reports and summaries; watching TV programs and movies related to the health sciences; attending health-related lectures and workshops; belonging to a health science club, health guild or professional organization; actively supporting health care expansion and medical research drives.

Skills

- Ability to concentrate for long periods of time
- Ability to conduct and clearly explain scientific research
- Ability to make keen observations and appropriate decisions
- Ability to work under pressure and meet deadlines
- High proficiency for accuracy and detail
- Proficiency in observing, collecting, and analyzing scientific data
- Proficiency in reading, writing, speaking, and memorization
- General knowledge of health sciences
- Physical stamina, good vision, and manual dexterity
- Intellectual capacity to perform well in most undergraduate and graduate college programs
- Proficiency with computers

Values and Attributes

- Intellectual growth
- Achievement
- Wisdom
- Health
- Desire to help others and make a contribution to humanity
- Interest in public health and safety
- Sensitivity to the needs and pain of others
- Scientific inquiry
- Patience
- Self-discipline
- Thoroughness

Resources

- Damp, Dennis. *Health Care Job Explosion!: High Growth, Health Care Careers and Job Finder.* Bookhaven Press, 1998.
- Snook, Donald. *Opportunities in Health and Medical Careers.* VGM Career Horizons, 1998.
- **Academy of Students of Pharmacy**
  2215 Constitution Avenue
  Washington, DC 20037
  202-429-7595
  http://www.apha.org
  (keeps members informed about the profession and publishes "The Pharmacy Student," a quarterly newsletter)
- **American Academy of Physician Assistants**
  950 North Washington Street
  Alexandria, VA 22314
  703-836-2272
  http://www.aapa.org
  (provides information about careers, accredited programs, relationship with physicians, job opportunities and student membership)

Anthropology

Anthropology is the study of the origin and development of humanity. It attempts to provide students with a better understanding of human physical differences, language systems, and the way cultures today compare with cultures of the past Also covered is the study of animal development and how it compares with human development. Anthropology is divided into the following sub-branches: cultural anthropology, physical anthropology, linguistic anthropology, and archaeology.

High School Courses

Social Studies

Foreign Languages

Anthropology

Psychology

Geography

History

Sociology

Related Occupations

Anthropologist—-D

Archivist—-M/D

Bibliographer—-M

Curator—-M/D

Ethnologist—-M/D

Geographer—-B/D

Linguistic Anthropologist—-D

Paleontologist—-B/D

Social Worker—-M/D

Technical Writer—-B

Archaeologist—-M/D

Art Conservator—-B

Cultural Anthropologist—-D

Educator—-M/D

Genealogist——B/D

Historian—-M/D

Museum Worker—-V

Research Associate—-B

Sociologist—-D

Leisure Activities

Visiting libraries and museums; participating in historical preservation efforts; doing historical research; camping, backpacking, and exploring; participating in archeological field experiences; reading publications related to anthropology; joining an organization such as the American Anthropological Association; collecting relics, antiquities, and artifacts; working part-time or as a volunteer in an antique shop, museum, or college anthropology department; serving as a graduate research assistant.

Skills

- Background of general knowledge
- Aptitude for foreign language
- Intellectual capacity to perform well in most undergraduate and graduate programs
- Proficiency in reading comprehension, writing, and speaking
- Ability to conduct and explain scientific research clearly
- Good vision, spatial perception and manual dexterity
- Proficiency with computers
- Ability to accurately interpret and evaluate events, information, and ideas related to the past

Values and Attributes

- Achievement
- Appreciation for and understanding of other cultures
- Desire for recognition and to influence humanity
- Desire to research and explore the human past
- Interest in learning about the similarities and differences between cultures
- Patience
- Alertness
- Curiosity
- Resourcefulness
- Integrity
- Imagination

Resources

- **American Anthropological Association**
  4350 North Fairfax Drive, Suite 640
  Arlington, VA 22203
  703-528-1902
  http://www.ameranthassn.org/
  (provides job placement assistance and publishes *Careers in Anthropology*)
- **Society for American Archaeology**
  900 Second Street, NE #12
  Washington, DC 20002
  http://www.saa.org/
  (provides definition of archaeology, information about academic programs, careers, job opportunities, fieldwork, scholarships, student membership, and the informative booklet *Archaeology and You*)

Architecture

Architectural study includes design, construction, and development of both physical structures and elements of the natural environment. It exposes students to the combined skills of creative aesthetics and practical functionability. The field of architecture involves many responsibilities, including planning layout, drawing, research, design, making modifications, selecting materials and equipment, estimating time requirements and costs, determining specifications, supervision and inspection, and writing reports. The results of architectural design are evident in our houses, churches, office buildings, hospitals, airports, bridges, highways, parkways, recreational facilities, and community developments. Landscape architecture and naval architecture are two major specialties within this area.

High School Courses

Drawing	Architectural Drawing
Drafting	Blueprint Reading
Art Interior	Decorating
Sculpture	Math
Algebra	Geometry
Trigonometry	Calculus

Related Occupations

Aeronautical Drafters—-AA	Architect—-B/M
Architectural Drafter—-AA	Architectural Technician—-AA
Building Contractor—-V	Cartographer—-B
Civil Engineer—-B	Civil Engineering Technician—-AA
Commercial Artist—-AA/B	Computer Graphics Technician—-AA
Contractor Administrator—-B	Design/Building Specialist—-V
Drafter—-AA	Educator—-M/D
Graphic Designer—-AA	Illustrator—-V
Industrial Designer—-V	Interior Designer—-V
Landscape Architect—-V	Model Maker—-V
Structural Engineer—-V	Surveyor—-AA
Technical Illustrator—-AA	Technical Photographer—-AA/B
Technical Writer—-V	Urban Planner—-V/M

Leisure Activities

Taking art classes; drawing and sketching for fun; developing hobbies related to building models; working part-time or as a volunteer on a construction project or in an architectural firm; joining an architecturally related organization such as the Association of Student Chapters of the American Institute of Architects or the American Institute of Architects; reading publications related to architecture; doing jigsaw puzzles and playing games of strategy; designing house furniture and landscapes; taking elective courses like geometry, mechanical drawing, and blueprint reading; attending architecture-related lectures, workshops, trade shows, or conventions; serving as a student aide in a high school or college architecture department.

Skills

- Aptitude for accuracy and detail
- Ability to apply complex mathematical and engineering concepts to practical real-life problems
- Strong spatial and form perception
- Ability to work with others as well as alone for long periods of time
- Ability to make keen observations and appropriate decisions
- Aptitude for drawing and sketching
- Ability to recognize differences in shapes, shading, and color
- Intellectual capacity to perform well in most undergraduate or graduate college programs
- Ability to work under pressure and meet deadlines
- Aptitude for math
- Ability to communicate ideas both orally and in writing
- Ability to conduct and clearly explain scientific research

Values and Attributes

- Creativity
- Achievement
- Desire for recognition and appreciation from others
- Aesthetic awareness
- Ability to adapt to fluctuations and deadlines
- Ability to accept public scrutiny and criticism
- Analytical thought
- Imagination
- Artistic nature
- Practical mind
- Perseverance

Resources

- **American Institute of Architects**
  1735 New York Avenue, NW
  Washington, DC 20006
  202-626-7300
  http://www.e-architect.com
  (provides information about accredited schools, job placement service, internships, and career development)
- **American Society of Landscape Architects**
  636 I Street, NW
  Washington, DC 20001
  202-898-2444
  http://www.asla.org/
  (offers student membership, job placement assistance, and information about accredited schools)

Art

Art is the study of the various creative means of expressing human thoughts, interests, attitudes, emotions, and ideas. It involves both fine art and commercial art. Fine art study includes painting and drawing, sculpture, photography, printmaking, and crafts. Commercial art revolves around advertisement and includes design, illustration, film, videography, and TV, and the making of murals, cards, and posters. Art history, art education, advertising, art therapy, journalism, and public relations are other key areas of concentration. Some additional areas of specialization are ceramics, pottery, weaving, textile design, fashion design, jewelry design, interior decorating, and metalsmithing.

High School Courses

Art	Drawing
Art History	Watercolors
Painting	Sketching
Crafts	Pottery
Jewelry	Photography

Related Occupations

Antique Dealer—-V	Architect—-B
Archivist—-B	Art Appraiser—-B
Art Director—-B	Art Therapist—-B/M
Cartoonist—-AA/V	Cinematographer—-B/V
Computer Animator—-AA	Copywriter—-V
Curator—-M/D	Designer—-V/B
Educator—-B/D	Fashion Illustrator—-AA
Film Editor—-AA	Film Producer—-B
Florist—-V	Freelance Artist—-AA
Graphic Designer—-AA/B	Industrial Designer—-V
Interior Decorator—-A	Jeweler—-AA/V
Medical/Scientific Illustrator—-V	Model Maker—-V
Motion Picture Photographer—-V	Painter—-B/V
Photojournalist—-AA/B	Sculptor—-V
Sign Painter—-V	TV Director—-B/V

Leisure Activities

Entering art contests; working part-time or volunteering in an art studio, museum, or advertising agency; collecting art, jewelry, or crafts; working as a photographer or artist for a school newspaper; attending art shows, festivals, and art exhibits; collecting antiques; developing skills in weaving, sculpture, macrame, furniture restoration, or photography; freelance drawing and painting; sewing, knitting, and crocheting; making and editing movies; helping to develop advertising material for local community service organizations and other groups.

Skills

- Proficiency for accuracy and detail
- Ability to concentrate intensely for long periods
- Ability to communicate ideas and emotions creatively
- Ability to recognize difference in shapes, shading, and color
- Familiarity with computer-aided design (CAD) techniques
- Aptitude for spatial relationships
- Ability to meet deadlines
- Good finger and manual dexterity
- Ability to make keen observations and appropriate decisions

Values and Attributes

- Aesthetic awareness
- Independence
- Self-expression and personal fulfillment
- Desire to influence others
- Creativity
- Feel for design and form
- Ability to adjust to ups and downs
- Ability to adjust to close public scrutiny and criticism
- Imagination
- Curiosity
- Patience
- Perseverance
- Dedication
- Flexibility
- Self-discipline

Resources

- **National Art Education Association**
  1916 Association Drive
  Reston, VA 20191
  703-860-8000
  http://www.naea.reston.org/
  (provides information about careers, accredited schools, accrediting standards, and other resources)
- **Society of Illustrators**
  128 East 63rd Street
  New York, NY 10021
  212-838-2560
  http://www.societyillustrators.org/
  (offers student membership, scholarships, career tips, and other resources)

Astronomy

Astronomy, a branch of the physical sciences, involves the study of our universe—its origin, its physical properties, its changes, and the distribution of its physical phenomena. An astronomer observes the planets, sun, solar system, and galaxies and then analyzes, interprets, and reports the findings. Astronomy is closely associated with mathematics and is usually considered a subdivision of physics. Some related majors: Physics, Chemistry, Mathematics, Aeronautical Engineering, Geology, Earth Science, Meteorology, Solar Energy, Planetary Science, and Computer Science.

High School Courses

Science

Physical Science

Physics

Algebra

Trigonometry

Computer Science

EarthScience

Chemistry

Math

Geometry

Calculus

Related Occupations

Acoustical Engineer—-V

Aerospace Engineer—-B

Astronomer—-D

Biophysicist—-B/D

Computer Programmer—-V

Electrical/Electronics Engineer—-B

Geophysicist—-B/D

Metallurgical Engineer—-V

Mineralogist—-B/D

Optical Physicist—-B

Research Technician—-AA

Systems Analyst—-B

Acoustical Physicist—-B

Aerospace Engineering Technician—-AA

Astrophysicist—-B/D

Cartographer—-B

Educator—-B/D

Geologist—-V

Mathematician—-B/D

Meteorologist—-V/D

Oceanographer—-B/D

Radiographer—-V

Seismologist—-V

Leisure Activities

Visiting planetariums, observatories, and science museums; involvement in outdoor activities; attending science fairs and exhibits; joining a photography club, the Amateur Astronomers Association, The Webb Society, or other astronomy club; watching natural science programs on TV; doing lab experiments and projects; reading astronomy or science publications; working part-time or as a volunteer in a planetarium, observatory, campus astronomy department, or weather station; operating a ham radio; computer programming; radio/TV repair.

Skills

- Ability to analyze and solve quantitative problems and make appropriate decisions
- Proficiency in reading, writing, speaking, and memorization
- Ability to concentrate for long periods of time
- Aptitude for accuracy and detail
- Acute spatial and form perception
- Proficiency in mathematics
- Intellectual capacity to perform well in most undergraduate and graduate college programs
- Ability to conduct and clearly explain scientific research
- Good vision, finger dexterity, and mechanical ability
- Proficiency with computers
- Ability to make keen observations

Values and Attributes

- Achievement
- Independence
- Intellectual growth
- Recognition
- Tendency toward analytical and logical thinking
- Intellectual curiosity about the atmosphere, space, and universal phenomena
- Fondness for physics and mathematics
- Imagination
- Self-discipline
- Perseverance
- Patience
- Precision

Resources

- **American Astronomical Society**
  2000 Florida Avenue, Suite 400
  Washington, DC 20009
  202-328-2010
  http://www.aas.org
  (maintains job placement services and publishes a career brochure)
- **Astronomical League**
  2112 King Fisher Lane, East
  Rolling Meadows, IL 60008
  847-398-0562
  http://www.mcs.net/

Banking and Finance

Banking and finance is a major field in the area of business which involves the study of how money is stored, protected, received, distributed, and generally managed. Banking and finance is a broad area and tends to overlap with a number of more specialized fields such as securities and insurance. Study in this area focuses on methods of deposits and withdrawals, checking and savings accounts, loans, interest rates, credit, trusts, investments, accounting procedures, budgets and financing, and securities. Areas of specialization are numerous and include savings and loans, checking customer service, clerical, accounting, credit cards, computer systems, research, budget, expenditures and cost analysis, supervision and administration, trust services, and securities.

High School Courses

Math	Business Math
Consumer Math	Bookkeeping
Accounting	Computer Programming
Economics	

Related Occupations

Accountant—-V	Account Executive—-B
Actuary—-B/V	Advertising Manager—-V
Appraiser/Assessor—-B	Bank Economist—-B/D
Bank Teller—-V	Branch Manager—-B
Budget Accountant—-B	Computer Programmer—-B
Controller-Accountant—-B	Correspondent Banking Officer—-B
Cost Accountant—-B	Credit Analyst—-AA/B
Credit Manager—-AA/B	Educator—-B/D
Financial Aid Officer—-B	Financial Analyst—-B
Financial Planner—-B	Insurance Agent—-V/B
Internal Auditor—-B	International Banking Officer—-B
Investment Banker—-B	Loan Officer—-B
Securities Clerk—-AA/V	Statistician—-B
Stockbroker—-B	Systems Analyst—-B
Treasurer—-B	Trust Administrator—-V

Leisure Activities

Working as a part-time or volunteer treasurer or tax preparer; sitting on a financial advisory board; reading publications related to banking and finance; attending finance-related lectures, workshops, or conventions; participating in investment activities (real or virtual); solving problems involving analytical and logical processes; joining a professional organization such as the American Banking Association; working part-time in a bank, savings and loan agency, or credit union; serving as a student aide in an accounting or business department.

Skills

- Ability to organize, analyze, and interpret numerical data
- Aptitude for accuracy and detail
- Ability to make sound judgments and decisions and to solve quantitative problems
- Ability to explain complex financial transactions and data to others
- Proficiency with computers
- Proficiency in written and oral communication
- Ability to communicate to and get along with people of different personalities and backgrounds
- Knowledge of financial and economic history, practices, and trends

Values and Attributes

- Wealth
- Recognition and appreciation from others
- Achievement
- Good eyesight and emotional well-being
- Tendency to be organized, confident, and businesslike
- Ability to handle money
- Interest in working with both people and data
- Integrity
- Alertness
- Ambition
- Discretion
- Trustworthiness

Resources

- **American Bankers Association**
  1120 Connecticut Avenue, NW
  Washington, DC 20036
  800-338-0626
  http://www.aba.com
  (sponsors industry training and educational programs, including correspondence)
- **Credit Union National Association**
  PO Box 431
  Madison, WI 53701
  608-231-4000
  http://www.cuna.org
  (offers training assistance and employment listings and distributes information on various areas of credit union management)

Biology

Biology is the study of life, from the simplest forms of plants and animals (including one-celled animals and algae) to the highly complex structure of the human being. It includes the study of how organisms are structured as well as how they function and relate to each other. Among the major branches of biology are human anatomy and physiology, botany (the study of plants), microbiology (the study of microscopic organisms), zoology (the study of animals), and ecology (the study of the relationship between organisms and the environment). Interested students may elect to concentrate in one or more of the subdivisions associated with the major biological branches.

High School Courses

Science	Earth Science
Biology	Physiology
Zoology	Chemistry
Health	

Related Occupations

Biochemist—-B/D	Biologist—-B/D
Botanist—-B	Dietician—-V
Ecologist—-B/D	Educator—-B
Florist—-V	Food Scientist—-B
Forester—-B	Funeral Director—-AA/B
Geneticist—-B/D	Horticulturist—-B/D
Medical Illustrator—-V	Medical Lab Technician—-AA
Medical Librarian—-M/D	Microbiologist—-B/D
Mycologist—-D	Nutritionist—-B
Occupational Therapist—-B	Paramedic—-AA
Parasitologist—-D	Physical Therapist—-B
Physician—-P	Physiologist—-D
Public Health Director—-B	Research Assistant—-B/M
Respiratory Therapist—-AA	Taxonomist—-B
Veterinarian—-P	Zoologist—-B/D

Leisure Activities

Attending science exhibits, county and state fairs, and 4-H shows; participating in Camp Fire Girls, Bluebirds, or scouting; belonging to an environmental concerns group, the Humane Society, a health club, or a community social group; browsing in floral shops or nature centers; working part-time or as a volunteer in a greenhouse or nursery; YMCA/YWCA involvement; hiking, fishing, trapping, backpacking, or gardening; visiting zoos or museums; owning or caring for pets; reading science magazines, books, and other related publications; performing lab experiments; taking nature walks; bird-watching; developing hobbies or collections related to leaves, butterflies, trees, flowers, or other natural items.

Skills

- Ability to concentrate for long periods of time
- Ability to make keen observations and appropriate decisions
- Proficiency in reading, writing, thinking, questioning, analyzing, and problem solving
- Ability to operate scientific equipment
- Intellectual capacity to perform well in most undergraduate and graduate college programs
- Proficiency for accuracy and detail
- Ability to organize and maintain accurate records
- Proficiency in speaking and memorization
- Ability to conduct and clearly explain scientific research
- Good vision and manual dexterity
- Thorough knowledge of basic biological theories and practices

Values and Attributes

- Achievement
- Creativity
- Desire to help humanity
- Intellectual growth
- Precision
- Enthusiasm for exploring
- Spirit of scientific inquiry
- Strong interest in living organisms
- Diligence
- Endurance
- Interest in challenges
- Patience
- Perseverance

Resources

- Louise, Chandra B. *Jumpstart Your Career in Bioscience.* Peer Publications, 1998.
- **American Institute of Biological Sciences**
  AIBS Headquarters
  1444 I Street, NW, Suite 200
  Washington, DC 20005
  202-628-1500
  http://www.aibs.org
  (publishes various brochures and Bioscience Journal)
- **American Society for Microbiology**
  1325 Massachusetts Avenue, NW
  Washington, DC 20005
  http://www.asmusa.org
  (offers job placement service and publishes numerous microbiology-related periodicals)

Botany

Botany is a major branch of the biological sciences and involves the study of plants. Plant groups typically included are bacteria, algae, fungi, mosses, ferns, and conebearing and flowering plants. Botany focuses on plant growth, structure, function, classification, distribution, and reproduction. Within the field of botany are a number of specialized areas, including morphology (microscopic and macroscopic plant structure), horticulture (the cultivation of ornamental plants and fruit and vegetable crops), and forestry. Plant habitat and the relationship of plants to humans and to our general environment are other important areas of botanical study.

High School Courses

Science
Biology
Chemistry

Earth Science
Landscape Gardening
Physiology

Related Occupations

Agronomist—-B/D
Biochemist—-B/D
Cooperative Extension Worker—-B
Cytologist—-B/D
Ecologist—-B/D
Farmer—-V
Florist—-V
Forester—-V
Groundskeeper—-V
Landscape Gardener—-V
Nursery Manager—-V
Phycologist—-M/D
Range Manager—-AA/B
Silviculturist—-V
Taxonomist—-B
Wood Technologist—B

Bacteriologist—-B/D
Botanist—-B/D
Curator—-M/D
Dietitian—-B
Educator—-B/D
Farm Manager—-B/V
Food Scientist—-V
Geneticist—-B/D
Horticulturist—-B/D
Mycologist—-D
Nutritionist—-V
Plant Breeder—-V
Seed Analyst—-B
Soil Conservationist—-B/D
Virologist—-M/D

Leisure Activities

Visiting nature centers, botanical gardens, conservatories, farms, parks, and museums; attending flower shows and fairs; browsing through floral shops, 4-H exhibits, and science displays; hiking, exploring, camping, sightseeing, and nature photography; gardening, canning, and freezing; sailing, canoeing, and swimming; developing hobbies and collections related to flowers, leaves, house plants, or floral design; working part-time or as a volunteer in a greenhouse, nursery, state park, or camp; joining a science club, orchid club, or conservation group; reading science publications; supporting or participating in natural resource preservation efforts; undertaking nature studies or rural expeditions.

Skills

- Proficiency in observing, collecting, and analyzing data
- Physical stamina, good vision, and manual dexterity
- Ability to concentrate for long periods of time
- Proficiency in reading, writing, speaking, and memorization
- Ability to conduct and clearly explain scientific research
- Proficiency for accuracy and detail
- Intellectual ability to perform well in most undergraduate or graduate college programs
- Proficiency in problem solving and decision-making
- Thorough knowledge of general biology

Values and Attributes

- Aesthetic awareness
- Creativity
- Independence
- Intellectual growth
- Interest in public health and safety
- Fondness for outdoor activities
- Deep appreciation for nature
- "Green thumb"
- Thoroughness
- Perseverance
- Patience
- Curiosity
- Endurance

Resources

- **American Society for Horticultural Science**
  600 Cameron Street
  Alexandria, VA 22314
  703-836-2024
  http://www.ashs.org
  (provides job descriptions, job placement service, and scholarships)
- **Botanical Society of America**
  1735 Neil Avenue
  Columbus, OH 43210
  614-292-3519
  http://www.botany.org/
  (ask for *Careers in Botany* and *Botany for the Next Millennium*)

Business Administration and Management

The field of business administration and management involves the coordination, implementation, promotion, supervision, and directing of the activities of individuals, organizations, and businesses. Effective techniques of business management constitute the backbone of strong economic, political, and social systems at all levels. Study in this major exposes students to methods of operation, coordination, sales and marketing, finance and budget, personnel, property and equipment management/maintenance, and security. Other key areas of concentration are organization, leadership, planning, interpersonal communications, delegating, supervising community resources, employee organizations, and policy making/implementation.

High School Courses

Business	Business Law
Management	Economics
Accounting	Speech
Sociology	Psychology

Related Occupations

Accountant—-B	Advertising Executive—-B
Airport Manager—-B	Chamber of Commerce President—-B
Chief Executive Officer—-B	City Manager—-B
College Dean—-M/D	Comptroller—-B/M
Consultant—-B/D	Convention Manager—-B
Database Manager—-B	Department Store Manager—-B
Director of Career Placement—-B/M	Director of Food Services—-B
Hotel/Motel Manager—-B/V	Human Resources Manager—-B
Production Superintendent—-B	Public Relations Specialist—-B
Recreation Director—-B	Restaurant Manager—-AA/V
Sales Manager—-V	School Administrator—-M/D
TV Director—-V	Traffic Manager—-V
Warehouse Manager—-AA/V	Wholesaler—-B
YMCA/YWCA Director—-B	

Leisure Activities

Working part-time in a local business establishment; participating in oratory contests; writing, starting, or managing a part-time business endeavor; assisting in the planning of a civic or social event; playing games of strategy, competition, or achievement; attending lectures, workshops, and conferences related to business management; serving as a student aide in a college business department; participating in a management training program; serving as a volunteer in a social agency; belonging to a Junior Achievement Club or a professional business organization.

Skills

- Ability to clearly communicate ideas and concepts to others
- Proficiency in reading, writing, and speaking
- Ability to solve problems and make appropriate decisions
- Strong background in business, marketing, and human relations
- Proficiency in organizing, planning, coordinating, and directing activities
- Ability to inspire productivity and exact loyalty from others
- Ability to respond spontaneously and work well under pressure
- Intellectual capacity to perform well in most undergraduate and graduate college programs
- Aptitude for leadership
- Proficiency in interpersonal communication
- Proficiency with computers

Values and Attributes

- Achievement
- Wealth
- Prestige
- Willingness to work beyond expectations
- Tendency to be responsible, show initiative, and exercise patience
- Leadership
- Decisiveness
- Resourcefulness
- Diplomacy
- Integrity
- Ambition

Resources

- **American Management Association**

  60 Broadway

  New York, NY 10019

  212-586-8100

  http://www.amanet.org

  (sponsors educational forums to enhance business skills, publishes "how to" articles for managers and various helpful newsletters)

- **National Management Association**

  2210 Arbor Boulevard

  Dayton, OH 45439

  937-294-0421

  http://nmal.org

  (offers leadership training and mentoring opportunities)

Chemical Engineering

Chemical engineering is the study of the practical application of science and mathematics in the process, manufacturing, equipment design, and development related to raw and synthetic substances and energy in an economical and efficient manner. It entails involvement with products that affect nearly every aspect of life such as clothes, foods, fuels, drugs, plastics, glass, soaps, paints, paper, and much more. Areas of special concentration include plastics, petroleum, research and development, environmental control, food, energy, pharmaceuticals, and education.

High School Courses

Math	Algebra
Geometry	Trigonometry
Calculus	Science
Earth Science	Physical Science
Chemistry	Physics
Computer Science	

Related Occupations

Agricultural Engineer—-B	Agronomist—-B
Biochemist—-B	Ceramic Engineer—-B
Chemical Engineer—-B	Chemical Engineering Technician—-AA
Chemical Research Engineer—-B/D	Chemist—-B
Computer Science Engineer—-B	Consulting Engineer—-B/D
Electrical Engineer—-B	Environmental Engineer—-B
Fire Protection Engineer—-V	Food Scientist—-B
Geological Engineer—-B	Materials Handling Engineer—-B
Metallurgical Engineer—-B	Metallurgist—-B
Nuclear Engineer—-V	Petroleum Engineer—-B
Pharmacist—-B	Pharmacologist—-D
Plastics Engineer—-B	Safety Engineer—-B
Textile Engineer—-B	Toxicologist—-B/D

Leisure Activities

Performing lab experiments and doing science projects; attending science fairs, exhibits, and demonstrations; reading publications related to chemistry or engineering; working part-time or as a volunteer in a hospital, chemistry lab, engineering firm, science department, or pharmaceutical firm; joining a chemistry or engineering club or organization.

Skills

- High proficiency in mathematics and physical sciences
- Ability to analyze, organize, and interpret scientific data
- Ability to work well with others
- Ability to make keen observations and sound judgments
- Aptitude for accuracy and detail, spatial perception, and abstract reasoning
- Sensitivity to economic considerations and human needs
- Proficiency in an area of specialization and knowledgeable of current practices and trends
- Ability to conduct and clearly communicate scientific research
- Intellectual capacity to perform well in most undergraduate and graduate college programs
- Proficiency with computers

Values and Attributes

- Creativity
- Achievement
- Knowledge
- Desire to help others live better
- Sensitivity to the health and safety of others
- Desire to see ideas developed into practical use
- Curiosity
- Integrity
- Perseverance
- Responsibility
- Imagination

Resources

- Woodburn, John. *Opportunities in Chemistry Careers.* VGM Career Horizons, 1997.
- **American Chemical Society**
  1155 16th Street, NW
  Washington, DC 20036
  800-227-5558
  http://www.acs.org
  (offers career guidance, counseling, and employment help and conducts special programs for disadvantaged persons)
- **American Institute of Chemical Engineers**
  3 Park Avenue
  New York, NY 10016
  800-242-4363
  http://www.aiche.org
  (publishes *Chapter One,* a student quarterly which provides study tips, career information, and campus reports)

Chemistry

Chemistry is a major branch of the physical sciences and involves the study of substances and energy. It focuses on their composition, characteristics, changes, reactions, uses, and benefits and dangers to humanity. Major sub-branches within chemistry include inorganic and organic chemistry, analytical chemistry, applied chemistry, biochemistry, and physical chemistry. Chemistry is used to produce food, clothing, furniture, drugs, plastics, glass, paper, and electronic devices. Knowledge of chemistry is crucial to environmental protection efforts as well as to humanity's health and safety.

High School Courses

Foods	Cooking
Science	Earth Science
Physical Science	Chemistry
Math	Algebra
Geometry	Trigonometry

Related Occupations

Agronomist—-B	Anesthesiologist—-B
Biochemist—-B	Ceramic Engineer—-B
Chemical Engineer—-B	Chemist—-B/D
Consumer Protection Specialist—-B	Dietitian—-B
Educator—-B/D	Food & Drug Analyst—-B
Food Scientist—-B	Geneticist—-B
Geologist—-B	Industrial Health Engineer—-B
Internist—-P	Laboratory Analyst—-B
Metallurgist—-B	Nuclear Scientist—-B/D
Nutritionist—-B	Patent Examiner—-B/P
Pharmacist—-B	Pharmacologist—-D
Pharmacologist Sales Representative—-B	
Physicist—-B/D	Science Technician—-AA
Technical Writer—-B	Toxicologist—-B/D
Wood Scientist—-D	

Leisure Activities

Performing lab experiments and doing science projects; attending science fairs, exhibits, and demonstrations; reading chemistry and science-related journals; cooking; watching scientific TV programs; working part-time or as a volunteer in a hospital, chemistry lab, or pharmaceutical firm; joining a chemistry or science club.

Skills

- Good vision and manual dexterity
- Ability to conduct and clearly explain scientific research
- Aptitude for accuracy and detail
- Ability to organize, analyze, and interpret scientific data
- Proficiency in reading, writing, speaking, and memorization
- Ability to make keen observations and appropriate decisions
- Strong mathematical background
- Intellectual capacity to perform well in most undergraduate and graduate college programs
- Proficiency with computers

Values and Attributes

- Achievement
- Intellectual growth
- Public recognition
- Desire to help humanity
- Willingness to take risks
- Pleasure in learning new skills
- Sensitivity to the health and safety of others
- Patience
- Curiosity
- Integrity
- Flexibility
- Responsibility

Resources

- Woodburn, John. *Opportunities in Chemistry Careers.* VGM Career Horizons, 1997.
- **American Chemical Society**
  1155 16th Street, NW
  Washington, DC 20036
  800-227-5558
  http://www.acs.org
  (offers career guidance, counseling, and employment help, and conducts special programs for disadvantaged persons)
- **American Institute of Chemical Engineers**
  3 Park Avenue
  New York, NY 10016
  800-242-4363
  http://www.aiche.org
  (publishes *Chapter One,* a student quarterly which provides study tips, career information, and campus reports)

Civil Engineering

Civil engineering is the study of how mathematical and scientific knowledge, experience, and theory is practically, economically, and efficiently applied in the use of material and natural resources to design and supervise the building of structures and facilities. Students are familiarized with the techniques of constructing bridges, dams, roads, railways, airports, water disposal systems, buildings, pipelines, and more. The four main areas of civil engineering are structures, transportation, sanitation, and soils. Specialties include geotechnical, environmental, transportation, hydraulic, structural, and pipeline engineering.

High School Courses

Industrial Arts	Drawing
Drafting	Blueprint Reading
Architectural Drawing	Math
Algebra	Geometry
Trigonometry	Calculus
Science	Earth Science
Physical Science	Chemistry
Physics	

Related Occupations

Architect—-B	Architectural Engineer—-B
Civil Engineer—-B	Civil Engineer Technician—-AA
Construction Engineer—-B	Consulting Engineer—-B/M
Ecologist—-B	Environmental Engineer—-B
Geological Engineer—-B	Geologist—-B
Geotechnical Engineer—-B	Highway Engineer—-B
Hydraulics Engineer—-B	Hydrologist—-B
Industrial Engineer—-B	Mechanical Engineer—-B
Mining Engineer—-B	Petroleum Engineer—-B
Photogrammetrist—-B	Pipeline Engineer—-B
Public Works Engineer—-B	Research Engineer—-B/D
Safety Engineer—-B	Sanitary Engineer—-B
Structural Engineer—-B	Transportation Engineer—-B
Urban Planner—-B/M	

Leisure Activities

Participating in clubs or organizations that require you to make oral presentations and write reports; doing jigsaw puzzles and playing games of strategy; solving analytic and logic problems; reading publications related to civil engineering; becoming a member of a student or professional engineering organization; attending engineering-related lectures, workshops, or conferences; engaging in hobbies related to building and designing structures; working part-time or as a volunteer with an engineering or construction firm or in a college engineering department.

Skills

- Ability to analyze, organize, and interpret scientific data
- Ability to work well with others
- Ability to make appropriate decisions and solve problems
- Ability to make keen observations and sound judgments
- Aptitude for accuracy and detail
- Proficiency in mathematics and science
- Proficiency in spatial perception and abstract reasoning
- Sensitivity to economic considerations and human needs
- Proficiency in an area of specialization and knowledge of current practices and trends
- Proficiency in written and oral communication
- Ability to conduct and clearly communicate scientific research
- Intellectual capacity to perform well in most undergraduate and graduate college programs
- Proficiency with computers

Values and Attributes

- Creativity
- Knowledge
- Desire to help others live better
- Achievement
- Ability to work on a team
- Enjoyment of challenges and the outdoors
- Interest in seeing ideas developed into practical uses
- Interest in moving from place to place
- Curiosity
- Alertness
- Flexibility
- Patience
- Responsibility
- Imagination

Resources

- Hagerty, Joseph and Louis Cohn. *Opportunities in Civil Engineering Careers.* VGM Career Horizons, 1997.
- **American Society of Civil Engineers**
  1801 Alexander Bell Drive
  Reston, VA 20191
  703-295-6000
  http://www.asce.org
- **JETS Guidance**
  1420 King Street, Suite 405
  Alexandria, VA 22314
  703-548-5387
  http://www.asee.org/jets
  (offers job placement listings, student membership, and scholarships, and sponsors student clubs)

Communications

Communications is the branch of language arts which focuses on the comprehensive expression of sound and visual, oral, and written symbols. Study in communications is geared toward understanding the many ways human beings develop, collect, disseminate, and transfer information through symbols, particularly via the mass media. Also included are the various ways in which communication serves to inform, persuade, entertain, and control. Communication is involved in almost everything we do and ranges from the simplest nonverbal communication efforts to the complex electronic messages of computers. Major areas of specialization include journalism, telecommunications, film, TV, radio, and advertising.

High School Courses

English	Technical English
Speech	Drama
Debate	Journalism
Theater	Writing

Related Occupations

Account Executive—-B	Actor/Actress—-V/B
Advertising Worker—-B	Announcer—-AA/B
Arbitrator—-B	Auctioneer—-V
Broadcast Technician—-AA	Columnist—-B
Commentator—-B	Copyeditor—-B
Copywriter—-B	Disc Jockey—-V
Editor—-B	Educator—-B/D
Foreign Correspondent—-B	Journalist—-B
Lecturer—-B	Lobbyist—-B
Media Specialist—-B/V	Music Director—-B
News Photographer—-AA/B	Online Content Developer—-B
Producer (Film, TV)—-B	Proofreader—-V
Public Relations Specialist—-B	Publisher—-B
Reporter—-B	Research Library Technician—-AA
Speech Writer—-B	Technical Writer—-B
TV Director—-B	Video Engineer—-V/B

Leisure Activities

Participating in local theater productions; attending movies, stage productions, lectures, or readings; working part-time or as a volunteer for a radio or TV station, printing, or publishing firm, department store, or advertising agency; participating on a debate or forensic team; serving as an announcer or editor of a small newspaper, magazine, or newsletter; joining a yearbook staff or broadcasting or drama club; visiting libraries; competing in writing or oratory contests; fundraising; reading professional publications; participating in election campaigns; working as a student assistant in a language arts or communications department; freelance writing.

Skills

- Ability to analyze, interpret, and appropriately convey physical and social events and behaviors to others
- Ability to meet deadlines and work under pressure
- Ability to read accurately and analytically
- Ability to relate to people of varying backgrounds
- Ability to respond quickly to unexpected circumstances
- Ability to solve problems and make decisions
- Background of general knowledge
- Good listening, clarifying, questioning, and responding skills
- Comprehensive command of grammar
- High proficiency in written and oral communication

Values and Attributes

- Creativity
- Desire for recognition and to influence others
- Independence
- Intellectual growth
- Poise and composure under close public scrutiny and criticism
- Appreciation for clear and stimulating communication
- Pleasant and friendly attitude
- Imagination
- Integrity
- Self-confidence
- Tactfulness
- Versatility

Resources

- Ellis, Elmo I. *Opportunities in Broadcasting Careers.* VGM Career Horizons, 1998.
- Noronha, Shonan. *Careers in Communication, New Edition.* VGM Career Horizons, 1998.
- *What Can I Do Now? Preparing for a Career in Journalism.* Ferguson Publishing Company, 1998.
- *What Can I Do Now? Preparing for a Career in Radio and Television.* Ferguson Publishing Company, 1998.

Computer Science

Computer study focuses on the design, manufacture, application, and effectiveness of computers, computer materials, and computer equipment. It includes the management, analysis, and dissemination of information via computer. From tiny hand-held electronic devices to huge multiterminal computer networks, computers pervade our culture and affect nearly every aspect of our daily lives.

High School Courses

Word Processing	Computer Programming
Computer Science	English
Algebra	Geometry
Trigonometry	Statistics

Related Occupations

Chief Information Officer—-B	Computer-Aided Designer—-AA/B
Computer Animator—-AA	Computer Applications Engineer—-B
Computer Operator—-AA/B	Computer Programmer—-V/B
Computer Science Engineer—-M/D	Computer Security Specialist—-B
Computer Service Technician—-AA	Database Analyst—-B
Database Manager—-B	Data-Entry Equipment Operator—-AA
Data Processing Department Manager—-B	
Educator—-B/D	Electronic Data Processing Auditor—-B
Hardware Salesperson—-AA/B	Hardware Service Person—-AA/B
Operations Manager—-AA/B	Robotics Technician—-AA
Software Engineer—-B	Software Package Developer—-B
Software Package Marketer—-B	Software Salesperson—-AA/B
Statistician—-B	Systems Analyst—-B
Systems Consultant—-B	Systems Manager—-B
Technical Support Technician—-V	Technical Writer—-B
Webmaster—-V	Word Processor—-AA

Leisure Activities

Working with a personal computer; working part-time or as a volunteer in a computer store, computer firm, or computer science department; repairing electronic appliances and other mechanical gadgetry; writing, score-keeping, or practicing electronics as a hobby; doing puzzles and playing games of strategy; browsing the Internet; solving analytic and logic problems; joining a computer club or organization; reading computer publications.

Skills

- Ability to cope with constant change
- Ability to analyze, make appropriate decisions, and solve problems
- Tendency toward logical thinking
- Ability to organize
- Proficiency in writing and speaking
- Aptitude for abstract reasoning, keen observation, and intense concentration
- Ability to work with others
- Proficiency with computers
- Proficiency for accuracy and detail
- Computational ability (using algebra for technician areas and using calculus for computer science areas)
- Ability to work under pressure
- Ability to understand and practically apply information derived from technical manuals and related materials

Values and Attributes

- Achievement
- Continuous intellectual growth
- Curiosity and enthusiasm for gadgetry
- Sense of responsibility
- Sensitivity to multiple perspectives
- Objectivity
- Perseverance
- Creativity
- Patience
- Thoroughness

Resources

- Eberts, Marjorie. *Careers for Computer Buffs and Other Technological Types, New Edition.* VGM Career Horizons, 1998.
- Jefferis, Davies. *Cybercareers.* Crabtree Publication Company, 1998.
- **Information Technology Association of America**
  1616 North Fort Meyer Drive, Suite 1300
  Arlington, VA 22209
  703-522-5055
  http://www.itaa.org
  (ask for the booklet entitled *Careers in Information Technology*)
- **Institute of Electrical and Electronic Engineers Computer Professionals**
  1730 Massachusetts Avenue, NW
  Washington, DC 20036
  202-371-0101
  http://www.computer.org
  (sponsors scholarships, offers student memberships, and publishes numerous computer-related materials)

Construction

Construction study concentrates on the building trades industry and involves learning about the structural, technical, and finishing aspects of construction, renovation, and maintenance on buildings, highways, industrial structures, systems, and utilities installations. Construction is a vast area and includes many specialties. A few of these are masonry, carpentry, heavy equipment operation, plumbing, electricity, bricklaying, contracting, roofing, painting, and insulation.

High School Courses

Woodworking
Physical Education
Blueprint Reading
Architectural Drawing
Algebra
Applied Math

Industrial Arts
Health
Drafting
Math
Geometry

Related Occupations

Bricklayer—-V
Carpenter—-V
Concrete Mason—-V
Drywall Applicator—-V
Estimator—-A/B
General Superintendent—-B/V
Insulation Worker—-V
Job Superintendent—-B/V
Operating Engineer—V
Paperhanger—-V
Plasterer—-V
Project Manager—-B/V
Roofer—-V
Sheet Metal Worker—-V
Terrazzo Worker—-V

Building Manager—-AA/V
Carpet Installer—-V
Construction Engineer—-B/V
Electrician—-V
General Contractor—-B/V
Glazier—-V
Ironworker—-V
Marblesetter—-V
Painter—-V
Pipefitter—-V
Plumber—-V
Rigger—-V
Safety Engineer—-B
Stone Mason—-V
Tilesetter—-V

Leisure Activities

Working part-time or as a volunteer worker with a construction firm, landscape gardening center, on a farm, or in various outdoor physical activities; building and repairing items as a hobby; reading manuals and books related to construction; engaging in outdoor sports and games which involve physical stamina, strength, and endurance; renovating and decorating your own home or yard; becoming a member of an organization such as the scouts or 4-H.

Skills

- Ability to work in awkward positions and at times in dangerous situations
- Physical stamina and good health, vision, and motor coordination
- Mechanical aptitude
- Finger dexterity
- Aptitude for accuracy and detail
- Proficiency in math
- Ability to read and interpret blueprints, specifications, diagrams, and schematic drawings
- Ability to meet deadlines
- Ability to make sound judgments, appropriate decisions, and solve problems
- Ability to follow direction and work alone as well as with others
- General knowledge of building trade organizations, practices, and trends
- Thorough knowledge and ability in an area of specialization

Values and Attributes

- Security
- Accomplishment
- Desire to make a contribution to society
- Willingness to work outdoors and in uncomfortable weather
- Ability to adjust to hazardous environments
- Enjoyment of hands-on activities
- Thoroughness
- Patience
- Precision
- Courage
- Resourcefulness
- Carefulness

Resources

- Wood, Robert. *Opportunities in Electrical Trades.* VGM Career Horizons, 1997.
- **Associated Builders and Contractors**
  1300 North 17th Street
  Rosslyn, VA 22209
  703-812-2000
  http://www.abc.org
  (sponsors management education programs as well as craft, apprenticeship, and skill training programs)
- **National Association of Home Builders**
  1201 15th Street, NW
  Washington, DC 20005
  202-822-0200
  http://www.nahb.com
  (exposes interested students to emerging housing technologies)

Culinary Arts

Culinary arts is the art, science, and business of cooking, baking, and preparing foods and beverages of all types for public and private institutions, agencies, and eating establishments. It exposes the student to the practices and techniques of quantity and fine food preparation as well as presentation, food storage, customer service, budgeting, purchasing, equipment use, recipe/menu development and use, sanitation, employee supervision, management, and governmental regulations. A few of the major specialities are bakery, pastry, buffet catering, meat cookery, cold meat and seafood preparation, soups and stocks, salads, vegetables, fish and shellfish, and sauces.

High School Courses

Foods	Cooking
Home Economics	Health
Baking	Chemistry

Related Occupations

Baker—-AA/V	Broiler Cook—-V
Butcher—-V	Caterer—-V
Chef—-V	Coffee Maker—-V
Cook—-V	Dietitian—-B
Executive Chef—-V	Food Scientist—-B
Food Service Supervisor—-B/V	Kitchen Manager—-V
Meatcutter—-V	Nutritionist—-B
Pastry Chef—-V	Restaurant Owner—-V/B
Salad Maker—-V	Sandwich Maker—-V
Sous Chef—-V	Technical Writer—-B

Leisure Activities

Attending lectures, clinics, and workshops related to food preparation; working part-time or as a volunteer in a school or community cafeteria or restaurant; baking for church or home; reading publications related to culinary arts; joining an organization such as the American Culinary Federation; entering baking or food contests; attending conventions, trade shows, or fairs that highlight culinary interests; engaging in a part-time food endeavor.

Skills

- Good motor skills, manual dexterity, and eye-hand coordination
- Good health and vision
- Ability to read and interpret recipes and menus
- Ability to meet deadlines and work well under pressure
- Ability to clearly communicate and understand others
- Ability to see and feel differences among shapes, shading, colors, and textures
- Ability to work well alone and with others
- Ability to adapt well to extreme temperature, noise, and odor variations
- Proficiency for accuracy and detail
- Ability to stand or sit in uncomfortable positions for extended periods of time
- Ability to cope with frequent change and variety
- Good mental and emotional well-being
- Keen sense of taste, smell, and touch
- Ability to organize and coordinate activities

Values and Attributes

- Desire for recognition and appreciation from others
- Achievement
- Creativity
- Strong interest in cooking and baking
- Tendency to maintain good health habits
- Willingness to work long and irregular hours and on weekends
- Dedication
- Perseverance
- Resourcefulness
- Flexibility
- Tactfulness
- Cleanliness

Resources

- Donovan, Mary. *Opportunities in Culinary Careers*. VGM Career Horizons, 1998.
- Masi, Mary. *Culinary Arts Career Starter*. Learning Express, 1999.
- **American Culinary Federation**
  10 San Bartola Drive
  St. Augustine, FL 32085
  904-824-4468
  (sponsors apprenticeship programs, provides information about certification and accreditation, and publishes student guide)
- **National Restaurant Association**
  Educational Foundation
  1200 17th Street, NW
  Washington, DC 20036
  202-331-5900
  http://www.restaurant.org
  (offers information about scholarships, career assistance, and schools)

Economics

Economics is the study of the production, consumption, and distribution of goods and services. Economics study attempts to clarify how the use of natural, technological, and financial resources affects the lives of human beings. Economic concerns can range from the study of how a poor Appalachian family survives financially to the complex study of international trade laws between nations. Topics of specialization are many and include the study of energy costs, business cycles, employment and unemployment, housing, health care, money policies, taxation, labor contracts, agriculture, and international trade.

High School Courses

Math	Business Math
Consumer Math	Bookkeeping
Accounting	Economics

Related Occupations

Account Executive—-B	Actuary—-B
Appraiser/Assessor—-V	Auditor—-B
Bank Officer—-AA/B	Buyer—-B
Controller—-B	Cost Accountant—-B
Credit and Loan Worker—-AA	Economist—-B/D
Educator—-B/D	Financial Planner—-B
Foreign Service Officer—-B	Home Economist—-B
Insurance Agent—-V/B	Internal Revenue Agent—-B
Labor Relations Specialist—-B	Manpower Director—-B
Market Research Analyst—-B	Real Estate Agent—-V
Sales Manager—-B	Sales Representative—-AA
Securities Analyst—-B	Statistician—-B
Stockbroker—-B	Tax Preparer—-B
Technical Writer—-B	Trust Administrator—-B
Urban Planner—-B	

Leisure Activities

Working as a part-time or volunteer cashier, treasurer, pollster, or salesperson; joining an international club or Junior Achievement group; participating in fundraising events; joining a professional economics organization; reading economics-related publications; joining an investment club; solving budgetary problems; bartering; writing reports or serving as a research assistant or student aide in an economics department; running a part-time business; joining a financial advisory board.

Skills

- Ability to conduct and clearly explain scientific research
- High proficiency in written and oral communication
- Strong background in economic theory and econometrics
- Ability to explain complex concepts and theories to others
- Thorough knowledge of statistical procedures
- Ability to collect and organize data
- Ability for accuracy and detail
- Ability to make keen observations and appropriate decisions
- Ability to solve problems and make sound predictions
- Intellectual capacity to do well in most undergraduate and graduate college programs
- Proficiency with computers

Values and Attributes

- Achievement
- Intellectual growth
- Security
- Ability to adjust to frequent changes
- Fondness for research and detail
- Interest in economic and fiscal trends
- Dependability
- Patience
- Objectivity
- Resourcefulness
- Perseverance
- Curiosity

Resources

- **American Marketing Association**

  250 South Wacker Drive

  Chicago, IL 60606

  312-648-0536

  http://www.ama.org

  (provides career bibliography and brochure entitled *Invest in Your Future,* offers student membership, and publishes student newsletter)

- **National Association of Business Economists**

  1233 20th Street, NW, Suite 505

  Washington, DC 20036

  202-463-6223

  http://www.nabe.com

  (publishes *Careers in Business Economics* and *the NABE Salary Survey* and offers employment opportunities and student membership)

Education

Education is the study of how human beings teach, learn, and develop knowledge, values, skills, and character qualities. The survival and success of societies, groups, and individuals hinges on effective education. Education takes place, either formally or informally, from the time one is born until the moment he or she dies. Study in this field is virtually unlimited and can include infant care, child psychology and adolescent education, preschool, elementary and secondary education, adult and parent education, education of the elderly, education of those who are handicapped and disadvantaged, military and employee education, and so on. A few of the major specializations are elementary, secondary, higher, adult and continuing, special, educational administration and supervision, preschool, guidance and counseling, testing and evaluation, business, industrial arts, and vocational/technical.

High School Courses

English
Math
Social Studies
History
Interpersonal Communications
Philosophy
Economics

Public Speaking
Science
Sociology
Psychology
Management
Religious Studies

Related Occupations

Adult and Vocational Education Teacher—-B

Adult Education Teacher—-B

Christian Education Worker—-B/P

College Professor—-M/D

Director of Admissions—-M

Director of Guidance—-M/D

Education Consultant—-M/D

Financial Aid Director—-M

Librarian—-M

Preschool Teacher—-B

Registrar—-M

School Superintendent—-M/D

Social Worker—-M

Teacher (ESL)—-B

Tutor—-B

Assistant Principal—-M

College Dean—-D

Counselor—-B/M

Director of Career Placement—-M/D

Director of Student Affairs—-B

Elementary School Teacher—-B

4-H Agent—-B

Personnel Director—-B

Principal—-B

School Psychologist—-M/D

Secondary School Teacher—-B

Special Education Teacher—-B/M

Teacher Aide—-AA

Vocational Rehabilitation Counselor—-M

Leisure Activities

Working part-time or as a volunteer in a preschool, nursery, elementary or secondary school; participating on a debate or forensic team, in oratory contests, or in a student organization; playing team sports or participating in community service organizations; serving as a Sunday school, children's church, or vacation Bible school teacher; reading educational publications; attending lectures, workshops, or conventions related to education; helping to organize and plan social or political events; working part-time or as a volunteer peer counselor, tutor, 4-H, or scout leader.

Skills

- Ability to persuade and influence others
- Proficiency in interpersonal communications
- Intellectual capacity to perform well in most undergraduate and graduate programs
- Broad background of knowledge
- Ability to organize and maintain accurate records
- Proficiency in one or more specialized areas
- Ability to solve problems and make appropriate decisions
- Aptitude for leadership
- Ability to maintain composure in stressful situations
- Understanding of educational theories and practices
- Ability to communicate ideas, facts, and abstract concepts to others
- Ability to relate to and interact with people of different personalities and backgrounds

Values and Attributes

- Desire to help others to learn and succeed
- Achievement
- Recognition and appreciation from others
- Intellectual growth
- Enjoyment of working and being with people
- Fondness for and dedication to human potential
- Sensitive, warm, friendly attitude
- Thirst for knowledge and understanding
- Patience
- Endurance
- Integrity
- Enthusiasm
- Tactfulness
- Objectivity
- Kindness

Resources

- Beers, Burt. et al. *Inside Secrets of Finding a Teaching Job.* JIST Works, 1997.
- Edelfelt, Roy, Ed.D. *Careers in Education: Third Edition.* VGM Career Horizons, 1998.
- **American Vocational Association**
  1410 King Street
  Alexandria, VA 22314
  800-826-9972
  http://www.avaonline.org/
- **National Council for Accreditation of Teacher Education**
  2010 Massachusetts Avenue, NW, Suite 500
  Washington, DC 20036
  202-466-7496
  http://www.ncate.org/
  (promotes and evaluates quality standards for educators on all levels and publishes a list of accredited schools)
- **National Education Association**
  1201 16th Street, NW
  Washington, DC
  202-833-4000
  http://www.nea.org/

Electrical/Electronic Engineering

Electrical/electronic engineering is the study of the practical application of mathematics and science in the production, control, distribution, and uses of electricity as well as the research, design, development, testing, and supervision of the manufacture of electronic equipment. Electrical/electronic engineering is an extremely large branch of engineering and ranges from the design of tiny electrical circuits to the construction of large electrical power plants. The four major branches of electrical engineering are communication, control systems, electronics, and power. Students may concentrate in the areas of electronic controls, radio, electromechanics, machine design, or construction.

High School Courses

Electricity	Electronics
Radio/TV Repair	Blueprint Reading
Math	Algebra
Geometry	Trigonometry
Calculus	Statistics
Computer Science	Science
Chemistry	Physics

Related Occupations

Acoustical Engineer—-B	Aeronautical Engineer—-B/D
Biomedical Engineer—-B	Circuit Engineer—-B
Communications Engineer—-B	Computer Science Engineer—-B
Consulting Engineer—-B/M	Control Engineer—-B
Electrical Engineer—-B	Electrical Engineering Technician—-AA
Electrician—-V	Electronics Instructor—-B
Environmental Engineer—-B	Field Service Engineer—-B
Fire Protection Engineer—-B	Illuminating Engineer—-B
Mechanical Engineer—-B	Nuclear Engineer—-B
Physicist—-B/D	Radio Engineer—-B
Safety Engineer—-B	Technical Writer—-B
Transmissions Engineer—-B	Video Recording Engineer—-V

Leisure Activities

Reading publications related to electricity and engineering; attending lectures and conferences related to engineering; repairing electrical items around the house; developing hobbies and interests related to electronic games and equipment; building models; belonging to a club or organization related to electrical engineering; working part-time or as a volunteer in an electronics shop, electrical firm, radio/TV repair shop, or college engineering department; participating in clubs or organizations that require you to make oral presentations and write reports.

Skills

- Proficiency with computers
- Proficiency in mathematics and physical sciences
- Ability to analyze, organize, and interpret scientific data
- Ability to work well with others
- Ability to make keen observations and sound judgments
- Aptitude for accuracy and detail, spatial perception, and abstract reasoning
- Sensitivity to economic considerations and human needs
- Proficiency in an area of specialization and knowledge of current practices and trends
- Ability to conduct and clearly communicate scientific research
- Intellectual capacity to perform well in most undergraduate college programs

Values and Attributes

- Achievement
- Creativity
- Knowledge
- Desire to help others live better
- Interest in challenges
- Enthusiasm for developing ideas and concepts in a practical way
- Imagination
- Dependability
- Patience
- Perseverance
- Conscientiousness
- Curiosity

Resources

- **American Society for Engineering Education**
  1818 N Street NW, Suite 600
  Washington, DC 20036
  202-331-3500
  http://www.asee.org
  (sponsors internships, offers student membership, and publishes guide to schools)
- **Institute of Electrical and Electronic Engineers**
  445 Hoes Lane
  Piscataway, NJ 08855
  732-881-0060
  http://www.ieee.org/
  (offers student memberships, information about accreditation, and a student career Web site which includes career planning, overviews, professional profiles, and salary surveys)
- **JETS**
  1420 King Street, Suite 405
  Alexandria, VA 22314
  703-548-5387
  http://www.asee.org/jets
  (offers job placement listings, scholarships, student membership, and student clubs)

Electrical/Electronics Technology

Electrical and electronics technology is the application of scientific theories and principles in the design, production, installation, testing, service, use, and control of electrical and electronic parts, equipment, and systems. Students in this area are exposed to theory and history, applied mathematics, testing measurement, circuitry, construction, currents and voltage, safety, pneumatics and electronic instruments, instrumentation, maintenance and repair, and much more. Specialties in this area are many and include instrumentation, construction electricity, robotics, broadcast communications, industrial electronics, radio/TV, radar, automated equipment, and digital technology.

High School Courses

Electricity	Electronics
Small Engine Repair	Radio/TV Repair
Blueprint Reading	Math
Applied Math	Algebra
Geometry	Trigonometry
Science	Physical Science

Related Occupations

Aircraft Electronics Technician—-AA	Audio and Sound Specialist—-AA
Automated Equipment Technician—-AA	
Biomedical Technician—-AA	Broadcast Technician—-AA
Electrical Appliance Repairer—-V	Electrical Engineering Technician—-AA
Electrical Technician—-AA	Electronic Equipment Salesperson—-V
Electronics Instructor—-B	Electronic Systems Tester—-AA
Electronics Technician—-AA/V	
Industrial Electronics Maintenance Worker—-AA	
Instrumentation Technician—-AA	Marine Electronics Specialist—-AA
Photo-optics Technician—-AA	Quality Control Technician—-AA
Radar Technician—-AA	Radio and Electrical Inspector—-B
Radio Repairer—-V	Robotics Technician—-AA
Technical Writer—-B	TV Technician—-AA

Leisure Activities

Reading publications related to electricity or electronics; repairing electrical items around the house; developing hobbies and interests involving electronic games and equipment; building models; belonging to an electronics club or related organization; working part-time or as a volunteer in an electronics shop, electrical firm, or radio/TV repair shop.

Skills

- Ability to understand and apply scientific theories and principles
- Ability to read, interpret, and follow directions, schematic drawings, diagrams, and blueprints
- Eye-hand coordination
- Aptitude for accuracy and detail
- Ability to concentrate intensely and work alone for long periods of time
- Ability to make keen observations and solve problems
- Spatial perception and proficiency in color coordination
- Finger and manual dexterity
- Aptitude for working with electronics and mechanics
- Proficiency in mathematics and physical science
- Ability to analyze, make sound judgments, and make appropriate decisions

Values and Attributes

- Independence
- Wisdom
- Achievement
- Enjoyment of hands-on work related to electrical gadgetry
- Enthusiasm for learning and applying new methods and techniques
- Patience
- Resourcefulness
- Conscientiousness
- Competence
- Thoroughness
- Dependability

Resources

- Basta, Nick. *Careers in High Tech.* VGM Career Horizons, 1998.
- Connelly, Robert. *Opportunities in Technical Education.* VGM Career Horizons, 1998.
- *Exploring Tech Careers.* Ferguson Publishing Company, 1998.
- **Electronics Technicians Association**
  604 North Jackson Street
  Greencastle, IN 46135
  765-653-4301
  http://www.eta.sda.com/
  (publishes tech-tips and employment monographs, sponsors community seminars, and offers certification information)
- **International Society of Certified Electronics Technicians**
  2708 West Berry, Suite 3
  Fort Worth, TX 76109
  817-921-9101
  http://www.iscet.com
  (offers training and testing programs for Certified Electronics Technicians)

English

English is a major branch of the language arts and its main focus is on the written word. However, a broader, more commonly accepted definition would include the study of literature, speech, and writing in all forms. The study of English orients students to the discipline of thinking. Students learn to critically evaluate their own speaking and writing—as well as the speaking and writing of others—and to express their thoughts and feelings coherently. They also learn how to edit their work and write for different audiences. The appropriate use and understanding of English is considered basic to everyday life and reflects a person's level of educational achievement. A few of the specialized areas within English are writing, literature, reading, and speech.

High School Courses

English
Literature
Poetry
Drama
Technical English
Public Speaking

Writing
Speech
Speed Reading
Debate
Business English
Forensics

Related Occupations

Actor/Actress—-B/V
Bibliographer—-B
Columnist—-B
Disc Jockey—-AA
Educator—-B/D
Interpreter/Translator—-B
Librarian—-M
Linguist—-M
Media Specialist—-B
Proofreader—-V
Reading Specialist/Consultant—-B
Secretary—-AA
Technical Writer—-B

Author—-B
Book Store Manager—-B
Copyeditor—-B
Editor—-B
Freelance Writer—-V
Journalist—-B
Library Technical Assistant—-AA
Lobbyist—-B
Playwright——B/V
Publisher—-B
Reporter—-B
Speech Writer—-B

Leisure Activities

Participating in local theater productions; attending movies, plays, lectures, or readings; freelance writing; providing a typing, tutoring, resume, or editing service; writing reports, papers, or poems; conversing with others; participating on a debate or forensics team, or in practical politics; editing or reporting for a small newspaper or newsletter; joining a yearbook staff; participating in a book club; visiting libraries; working part-time or as a volunteer for a high school or college radio or TV station; competing in writing or oratory contests; reading essays, articles, novels, short stories, plays, poetry, and professional journals.

Skills

- Background of general knowledge
- High proficiency in reading, writing, and speaking
- Comprehensive command of grammar and vocabulary
- Good listening, clarifying, questioning, and responding skills
- Ability to conduct and clearly explain research results
- Ability to read analytically
- Capacity to work well under pressure
- Ability to make keen observations and appropriate decisions
- Ability to concentrate for long periods of time

Values and Attributes

- Intellectual growth
- Independence
- Creativity
- Desire for recognition and to influence others
- Willingness to work toward a deadline
- Fondness for writing and/or speaking
- Self-discipline
- Tactfulness
- Integrity
- Imagination

Resources

- *What Can I Do Now? Preparing for a Career in Journalism.* Ferguson Publishing Company, 1998.
- **Dow Jones Newspaper Fund**
  PO Box 300
  Princeton, NJ 08053
  609-452-2820
  http://www.dowjones.com
  (publishes *Journalism Careers* and a scholarship guide, sponsors various internships and scholarships, and seeks to encourage careers in journalism)
- **Society for Technical Communication**
  901 North Stuart Street, Suite 904
  Arlington, VA 22203
  703-522-4114
  http://stc.org
  (offers information about technical communication schools and provides internships, scholarships, and several career brochures)

Food and Beverage Management/Service

Food and beverage management/service can be described as the art and business of managing and providing food services of all types for public and private institutions, agencies, and eating establishments. It includes the study of techniques in hospitality, hotel and restaurant maintenance, facilities, food purchasing and cost, food preparation and service, and front office operations. Other areas of focus are marketing, sanitation and safety, menu and nutrition, catering, and financial record-keeping.

High School Courses

Foods

Cooking

Health

Bookkeeping

Speech

Sociology

Food Service

Home Economics

Business Management

Sales

Psychology

Related Occupations

Assistant Restaurant Manager—-AA/V

Banquet Manager—-AA/V

Chef—-AA/V

Dining Room Attendant—-V

Executive Housekeeper—-B

Food and Beverage Director—-V

Food Service Manager—-V/B

Host/Hostess—V

Maitre d'Hotel—-V

Nutritionist—-B

Restaurant Manager—-AA/B

Steward/Stewardess—-V

Cafeteria Manager—-AA/V

Dietitian—-B

Director of Recipe—-V

Fast Food Worker—-V

Food Production Manager—-V

Home Economist—-B

Hotel/Motel Manager—-B

Merchandising Supervisor—-V

Purchasing Agent—-B

Sanitation/Maintenance Worker—-AA

Storeroom Supervisor—-V

Leisure Activities

Joining an organization such as the National Restaurant Association; working part-time or as a volunteer in a restaurant or hotel; planning or organizing community events that involve eating and/or serving; engaging in your own part-time food business endeavor; helping to organize, plan, and implement church or school picnics; reading publications related to food service or management; working part-time as a store cashier or manager; attending workshops, lectures, or conferences related to food service; hosting social events.

Skills

- Ability to solve problems and make appropriate decisions
- Aptitude for accuracy and detail
- Ability to follow directions and read and interpret menus
- Ability to work under pressure, maintain composure, and react spontaneously
- Ability to organize and coordinate activities
- Proficiency in interpersonal communication
- Ability to accept public scrutiny and criticism
- Ability to interact with people of different backgrounds and personalities
- Good health and vision
- Ability to work well with others
- Good motor skills, manual dexterity, and eye-hand coordination
- Familiarity with laws related to alcoholic beverages and minors

Values and Attributes

- Recognition and appreciation from others
- Desire to help others
- Creativity
- Achievement
- Pleasant and friendly personality
- Desire to serve and please others
- Willingness to work long and irregular hours and on weekends
- Sensitivity, poise, and integrity
- Persuasiveness
- Neatness
- Diplomacy
- Cleanliness
- Leadership
- Industriousness

Resources

- **American Culinary Federation**
  10 San Bartola Drive
  St. Augustine, FL 32085
  904-824-4468
  (sponsors an apprenticeship program, provides information about certification and accreditation, and publishes a student guide)
- **American Dietetic Association**
  216 West Jackson Boulevard, Suite 800
  Chicago, IL 60606
  312-899-0040
  http://www.eatright.org
  (provides career, employment, and scholarship information)
- **National Restaurant Association**
  1200 17th Street, NW
  Washington, DC 20036
  202-331-5900
  http://www.restaurant.org
  (offers information about scholarships, career assistance, and schools)

Foreign Language

Foreign language is a branch of the language arts that involves the study of languages other than one's native tongue. Studies in a foreign language improve students' ability to communicate, help them to develop cultural awareness and sensitivity, and expand their general knowledge. Proficiency in more than one language is becoming an increasingly valuable asset and enhances students' occupational possibilities as well as enjoyment of overseas travel. Foreign language courses are offered in most schools, colleges, and universities in the United States.

High School Courses

Foreign Language
English
History
Sociology
Latin
Speech
Anthropology

Related Occupations

Actor/Actress—-B/V
Anthropologist—-B/D
Civil Service Worker—-B
Customs Inspector—-AA
FBI/CIA Agent—-B/D
Flight Attendant—-AA
Foreign Service Officer—-B
Hotel Information Clerk—-V
Import/Export Clerk—-V
Journalist—-B
Maitre d'(hotel)—-AA/V
Proofreader—-V
Technical Writer—-B
Travel Agent—-AA

Announcer—-B
Bilingual Educator—-B/M
Copy Editor—-B
Diplomat—-B/M
Film Editor—-AA
Foreign News Correspondent—-B
Historian—-B/D
Hotel Manager—-AA/B
Interpreter/Translator—-B
Linguist—-M
Missionary—-B
Speech Pathologist—-B/M
Translator—-B
VISTA/Peace Corps Volunteer—-B

Leisure Activities

Traveling abroad; attending movies or participating in stage productions; visiting libraries; attending lectures and readings; working part-time or as a volunteer for Peace Corps, VISTA, or Red Cross International; joining a foreign language club; participating in oratory contests, student exchanges, or pen-pal experiences; working part-time or as a volunteer news announcer for a local radio or TV station, in a foreign language department, or in an ethnic restaurant; joining an international service organization such as the American Friends Service Committee or World Vision.

Skills

- Ability to make analogies
- Ability to practice for long periods of time
- Ability to adjust to new environments
- Ability to organize and memorize detailed information
- Background of general knowledge
- Comprehensive command of grammar and vocabulary
- Good listening, clarifying, and responding skills
- High proficiency in reading, speaking, and writing
- Proficiency in phonetics and ability to imitate sounds
- Tendency toward logical thinking

Values and Attributes

- Intellectual growth
- Appreciation for the culture and lifestyles of others
- Desire for peace and harmony
- Linguistic ability
- Adaptability
- Alertness
- Creativity
- Patience
- Self-discipline

Resources

- Camenson, Blythe. *Opportunities in Overseas Careers.* VGM Career Horizons, 1998.
- Rivers, Wilga, Ph.D. *Opportunities in Foreign Language Careers.* VGM Career Horizons, 1998.
- **American Institute for Foreign Study**
  102 Greenwich Avenue
  Greenwich, CT 06830
  800-727-2437
  http://www.aifs.org
  (sponsors exchange programs, study abroad, internships, and scholarships, and seeks to promote international understanding)
- **Modern Language Association of American**
  10 Astor Place
  New York, NY 10003
  212-614-6382
  http://www.mla.org/
  (promotes study and teaching of language and literature, has checklist for job seekers, and job market information)

Forestry

Forestry is concerned with the management, development, and use of forests and related areas. It involves the application of scientific methods as well as creative imagination. Forestry covers a broad spectrum and includes the care and maintenance of rangelands, grasslands, and brushlands. Study in this field includes wood science, forestry management, economics, conservation, fire protection and disease control, scaling, surveying, recreational use, research, and a number of other areas. Forestry overlaps with a number of fields including biology, physics, chemistry, and engineering. Among the many specializations are tree planting/harvesting, watershed management, wildlife management, forestry management, public recreation, fire control, disease and pest control, conservation, and wood science.

High School Courses

Science	Earth Science
Biology	Physical Science
Chemistry	Physics
Math	Algebra
Geometry	Trigonometry

Related Occupations

Agricultural Extension Worker—-B	Agronomist—-B
Botanist—-B	Ecologist—-B
Educator—-B/D	Farm Manager—-B/V
Forester—-B	Forestry Technician—-AA
Mycologist—-D	Naturalist—-B
Park Police—-AA/V	Park Ranger—-B
Plant Geneticist—-B	Rancher—-V
Range Manager—-AA/B	Seed Analyst—-B
Silviculturist—-B	Smoke Jumper —-V
Soil Conservationist—-B	Surveyor—-AA
Taxonomist—-B	Tree Nursery Manager—-V
Tree Surgeon—-V	Virologist—-B
Wildlife Manager—-B	Wood Technologist—-B

Leisure Activities

Visiting nature centers, botanical gardens, state and national parks, conservatories, camps, and museums; hiking, exploring, camping, sightseeing, backpacking, and collecting items related to nature; joining a professional organization such as the Society of American Foresters; subscribing to a science publication such as the *Journal of Forestry;* joining a forestry club or conservation group; supporting or participating in natural resource preservation efforts; undertaking nature studies or rural expeditions; working part-time as a park aide, forest aide, nursery worker, or nature tour guide.

Skills

- Physical stamina, good vision, and manual dexterity
- Ability to work alone and with little supervision
- Ability to conduct and clearly explain scientific research
- Ability to communicate well with others
- Proficiency in reading, writing, speaking, and memorization
- Ability to supervise and manage people and activities
- Intellectual ability to perform well in most undergraduate and graduate college programs
- Thorough knowledge of forestry and related areas
- Proficiency in problem solving and decision-making

Values and Attributes

- Independence
- Aesthetic awareness
- Desire to help humanity
- Intellectual growth
- Creativity
- Fondness for outdoor activities
- Desire to conserve and protect the natural environment
- Ability to endure sometimes challenging physical conditions
- Appreciation of nature
- Perseverance
- Desire for challenges
- Curiosity
- Responsibility
- Courage

Resources

- Coleman, Ronny. *Opportunities in Fire Protection Services.* VGM Career Horizons, 1997.
- Wille, Christopher. *Opportunities in Forestry.* VGM Career Horizons, 1998.
- **Society of American Foresters**
  5400 Grosvenor Lane
  Bethesda, MD 20814
  301-897-8720
  http://www.safnet.org
  (provides forestry facts and information about careers and accredited educational programs)
- **American Forests**
  PO Box 2000
  Washington, DC 20013
  202-955-4500
  http://www.amfor.org/
  (provides internships, promotes conservation, and publishes *American Forests* magazine)

Geography

Geography is the study of the interrelationships between the earth and its people; it is considered both a social and natural science. Geography focuses on climate, land, water, space, mineral resources, population density, changes in environment, and how humans adapt to them. Geographical study encompasses human geography, economic geography, physical geography, political geography, medical geography, regional geography, and educational geography.

High School Courses

Geography	World History
Physical Geography	Earth Science
Civics	Social Studies
Sociology	Government
Economics	

Related Occupations

Anthropologist—-D	Cartographer—-B
Cartographic Technician—-AA	Climatologist—-B
Computer Mapper—-B	Ecologist—-B
Educator—-B/D	Environmental Scientist—-B
Environmental Technician—-AA	Geographer—-B/D
Geologist—-B	Geomorphologist—-B/D
Geophysicist—-B/D	Historian—-B/D
International Economist—-B	Landscape Architect—-B
Market Research Analyst—-B	Meteorologist—-B
Oceanographer—-B	Petrologist—-B
Photogrammetric Technician—-AA	Photogrammetrist—-B
Photographer—-B	Research Assistant—-B/M
Seismologist—-B	Sociologist—-D
Soil Conservationist—-B	Surveyor—-AA/V
Urban Planner—-M/D	

Leisure Activities

Visiting natural science museums; involvement in outdoor activities; attending geographical seminars and conferences; watching TV shows related to the natural habitat; exploring and traveling; hiking, camping, and backpacking; reading or subscribing to professional publications; solving analytical and logical problems; joining organizations such as the American Geographical Society or the National Council for Geographic Education; working part-time or as a volunteer in an architectural firm, school geography department, or at an archeological site.

Skills

- Proficiency with computers
- Ability to understand and interpret maps, graphs, and charts
- Acute spatial and form perception
- Good vision and finger dexterity
- Thorough understanding of geographical principles and statistical techniques
- Proficiency in reading, writing, and speaking
- Ability to analyze, make appropriate decisions, and solve quantitative problems
- Ability to conduct and clearly explain scientific research
- Aptitude for accuracy and detail
- Intellectual capacity to perform well in most undergraduate and graduate college programs

Values and Attributes

- Achievement
- Intellectual growth
- Independence
- Desire to help and influence humanity
- Desire to help people understand and adapt to their environment
- Keen interest in both the natural and social sciences
- Spirit of scientific inquiry
- Curiosity
- Patience
- Persistence
- Resourcefulness

Resources

- **Association of American Geographers**
  1710 16th Street, NW
  Washington, DC 20009
  202-234-1450
  http://www.aag.org/
  (provides information about careers in geography)
- **National Geographic Society**
  PO Box 98199
  Washington, DC 20090
  800-647-5463
  http://www.nationalgeographic.com/
  (provides information for geography lovers; has a "Glad You Asked" department)

Geology

Geology is a major branch of the physical sciences which involves the study of the earth. Geology is divided into two main fields: physical geology (the study of earth matter and influencing forces) and historical geology (the history of the earth). Geology includes the study of rocks, soils, mountains, rivers, oceans, and caves. Study in geology also encompasses the exploration and production of mineral and energy resources. Sub-branches of geology include meteorology, climatology, oceanography, geophysics, petrology, sedimentology, stratigraphy, paleontology, mineralogy, and geochemistry.

High School Courses

Science	Earth Science
Physical Science	Geography
Chemistry	Physics
Math	Algebra
Geometry	Trigonometry

Related Occupations

Astronomer—-D	Cartographer—-B
Chemist—-B	Environmental Scientist—-B
Geodesist—-B	Geographer—-B/D
Geologist—-B	Geophysicist—-B/D
Hydrographer—-B	Hydrologist—-B
Laboratory Technician—-AA	Metallurgical Engineer—-B
Metallurgist—-B	Meteorological Technician—-AA
Mineralogist—-B/D	Mining Engineer—-B
Nuclear Engineer—-B/D	Oceanographer—-B/D
Paleontologist—-B/D	Petroleum Engineer—-B
Petrologist—-B	Pharmacist—-B
Photogrammetrist—-B	Physicist—-B/D
Seismologist—-B	Stratigrapher—-B
Surveyor—-AA	Technical Writer—-B

Leisure Activities

Visiting science museums; participating in outdoor activities; attending science fairs and exhibits; watching TV shows related to the natural habitat; exploring and traveling; hiking, mountain climbing, camping, and backpacking; doing jigsaw puzzles and playing games of strategy; joining a geology or archeological club; developing hobbies and collections related to soils, rocks, coins, jewelry, or other artifacts; reading science magazines.

Skills

- Intellectual capacity to perform well in most undergraduate and graduate college programs
- Ability to work with people of varied backgrounds
- Acute spatial and form perception
- Ability to make appropriate decisions and to solve quantitative problems
- Aptitude for accuracy and detail
- Proficiency in reading, writing, speaking, and memorization
- Ability to conduct and clearly explain scientific research
- Physical stamina, good vision, and manual dexterity
- Thorough knowledge of geological principles and mathematics
- Proficiency with computers

Values and Attributes

- Independence
- Intellectual growth
- Achievement
- Enthusiasm for exploration, travel, and outdoor work
- Spirit of scientific inquiry
- Resourcefulness
- Imagination
- Patience
- Determination
- Dedication

Resources

- Krueger, Gretchen. *Opportunities in Petroleum Careers.* VGM Career Horizons, 1999.
- **American Geological Institute**
  4220 King Street
  Alexandria, VA 22302
  703-379-2480
  http://www.agiweb.org
  (provides information about scholarships and careers, including career statistics and profiles of geoscientists)
- **Geological Society of America**
  PO Box 9140
  3300 Penrose Place
  Boulder, CO 80301
  303-447-2020
  http://www.geosociety.org
  (distributes information about careers in geoscience and employment opportunities)

Health Administration, Management, and Related Services

Health administration, management, and related services is concerned with the effective and efficient delivery of health care services to community residents. It involves the coordination and management of public and private hospitals, nursing homes, med-centers, clinics, mental health organizations, community health programs, and more. Study in this area concentrates on the business practices, leadership skills and support services employed by health care administrators and managers in their effort to identify, treat, prevent, and control disease, sickness, and injury. Students are exposed to the various strategies used to ensure a high quality of patient care service in a cost-effective manner. A few of the concentrations within this field are patient care, publicity, budget and finance, maintenance, housekeeping, personnel, food service and nutrition, employee relations, facilities and equipment, governmental regulations, benefits, and record-keeping.

High School Courses

Health	Business Management
Business Math	Consumer Math
Bookkeeping	Accounting
Economics	Speech
Psychology	Sociology

Related Occupations

Activities Supervisor—-B	Chief Dietitian—-B
Coordinator of Rehabilitation Services—-B/M	
Director of Volunteer Services—-B	
Emergency Medical Services Coordinator—-B	
Executive Housekeeper—-B	Health Consultant—-B/D
Health Information Specialist—-B	Health Services Administrator—-M
Hospital Comptroller—-B	Hospital Food Service Manager—-B
Hospital Personnel Director—-B	Hospital Records Administrator—-B
Information Specialist—-B/M	Medical Engineer—-B
Medical Records Administrator—-B	Nursing Home Director—-M
Occupational Safety and Health Inspector—-B	
Psychiatric Social Worker—-M	Public Health Educator—-B
Public Health Service Officer—-B	Public Health Statistician—-B
Public Relations Specialist—-B	Sanitary Engineer—-B

Leisure Activities

Reading publications related to health care services and management; attending lectures, workshops, and conferences related to health concerns; belonging to a health club or professional health organization; working part-time or as a volunteer in a hospital or nursing home, health agency, or business establishment; actively supporting health endeavors; joining a health advisory board; serving as a club or program officer.

Skills

- Ability to clearly communicate ideas and concepts to others
- Ability to inspire productivity and exact loyalty from others
- Aptitude for leadership
- Proficiency in interpersonal communications
- Proficiency in reading, writing, and speaking
- Knowledge of health care services, policies, and trends
- Intellectual capacity to perform well in most undergraduate and graduate programs
- Ability to solve problems and make appropriate decisions
- Proficiency in organizing, planning, coordinating, and directing activities
- Ability to meet deadlines and work well under pressure

Values and Attributes

- Desire to help others and make a contribution to humanity
- Health
- Achievement
- Prestige
- Willingness to work beyond expectations
- Strong interest in health care services
- Initiative
- Resourcefulness
- Decisiveness
- Diplomacy
- Integrity
- Responsibility

Resources

- *Exploring Health Care Careers.* Ferguson Publishing Company, 1998.
- **American College of Healthcare Executives**
  One North Franklin Street, Suite 1700
  Chicago, IL 60606
  312-424-2800
  http://www.ache.org/
  (offers description of trends and career planning tips and publishes list of health administration programs/schools)
- **Medical Group Management Association**
  104 Inverness Terrace East
  Englewood, CO 80112
  303-799-1111
  (offers scholarships, placement services, and career planning assistance)

History

History is the study of major social, political, cultural, and economic events of the past. Applying the results of historical study is important for the preservation and future growth of nations and institutions. Knowledge of the past enables individuals to develop pride and appreciation for the accomplishments of others. In addition, a thorough understanding of past problems and the strategies used to resolve them can help humans to plan their present and future lives more effectively. Historical study is normally divided into ancient, medieval, and modern.

High School Courses

History	World History
Civics	Government
Social Studies	Sociology
Anthropology	

Related Occupations

Anthropologist—-D	Archaeologist—-D
Archivist—-B	Curator—-B
Economist—-B	Educator—-B/D
FBI/CIA Agent—-B	Foreign News Correspondent—-B
Foreign Service Officer—-B/M	Freelance Writer—-B
Genealogist—-B/D	Gerontologist—-B
Historian—-B/D	Lawyer—-P
Librarian—-M	Market Research Analyst—-B
Newspaper Reporter—-B	Peace Corps Worker—-B
Political Scientist—-B/D	Public Administrator—-B
Research Assistant—-B	Technical Writer—-B
Writer—-V	

Leisure Activities

Traveling; visiting libraries and museums; collecting relics, stamps, antiques, or coins; working part-time or as a volunteer in a library, museum, historical society, or history department; maintaining a diary; viewing historical dramas or documentaries on TV or at a theater; joining a historical association or supporting historical preservation efforts; visiting book stores, antique shops, or flea markets; reading history-related publications, attending auctions or antique shows; participating in activities that involve research.

Skills

- Ability to accurately identify and evaluate records of past events, ideas, and facts
- Intellectual capacity to perform well in most undergraduate and graduate college programs
- Proficiency in reading comprehension, writing, and speaking
- Ability to conduct and clearly explain scientific research
- Ability to collect and organize important historical data
- Ability to concentrate for long periods of time
- Broad background of general knowledge
- Ability to make keen observations, solve problems, and make appropriate decisions
- Proficiency for accuracy and detail

Values and Attributes

- Appreciation for past events and accomplishments
- Independence
- Intellectual growth
- Recognition
- Strong interest in reading and writing
- Continuous desire to study and research the past
- Reluctance to throw anything away
- Analytical mind
- Objectivity
- Curiosity
- Resourcefulness
- Reflective nature
- Integrity
- Patience

Resources

- Marek, Rosanne. *Opportunities in Social Science Careers.* VGM Career Horizons, 1997.
- **American Historical Association**
  400 A Street, SE
  Washington, DC 20003
  202-544-2422
  http://www.theaha.org
  (offers information about the job market and careers and publishes articles on the benefits of studying history and becoming an historian)
- **Society of American Archivists**
  527 South Wells, 5th Floor
  Chicago, IL 60607
  312-922-0140
  http://www.archivists.org/
  (publishes employment bulletin with useful descriptions of the types of jobs available)

Home Economics

Home economics is concerned with the quality and efficiency of family life and home care. Study within this area covers a broad spectrum and overlaps with a number of related fields. The four major divisions of home economics are food and nutrition, family life and child care, clothing and textiles, and home management, decorating, and equipment. Key areas of concentration include consumer management, budget, education, recreation, housing, health, nutrition, and transportation.

High School Courses

Foods	Food Service
Cooking	Sewing
Clothing	Home Economics
Child Care	Health
Family Living	Consumer Math

Related Occupations

Buyer—-B	Child Care Worker—-AA
Child Welfare Case Worker—-B	Clothing Designer—-B
Cook/Chef—-AA/V	Cooperative Extension Worker—-B
Day Care Director—-AA/B	Department Manager—-B
Dietitian—-B	Director of Food Service—-B
Dressmaker—-V	Economist—-B
Executive Housekeeper—-B	Fashion Designer—-B
Food and Drug Inspector—-B	Food Scientist—-B
Food Service Manager—-V/B	Home Economist—-B
Home Health Aide—-V/C	Hotel/Motel Manager—-B
Interior Decorator—-B	Market Researcher—-B
Merchandise Displayer—-B	Nutritionist—-B
Purchasing Agent—-B	Sales Manager—-B
Social Service Aide—-AA	Social Worker—-B/M
Tailor—-V	Upholsterer—-V

Leisure Activities

Participating in charitable outreach endeavors; working part-time or as a volunteer in a day care center, hotel, hospital, or community service agency; reading publications related to homemaking; joining an organization such as 4-H or Future Homemakers of America; attending lectures, workshops, or conventions related to home economics; cooking; sewing; working part-time in a food, clothing, furniture, appliance, or hardware store; working as a student aide in a home economics department.

Skills

- Ability to organize, conduct, and clearly explain scientific research
- Ability to persuade and influence others
- Knowledge of community resources
- Proficiency in interpersonal communications
- Ability to communicate and interact with people of different backgrounds and personalities
- General knowledge in many areas
- Proficiency in speaking, writing, and listening
- Ability to analyze and think practically
- Ability to make keen observations, evaluations, and appropriate decisions
- A good understanding of human nature
- Ability to solve problems

Values and Attributes

- Helpfulness
- Achievement
- Creativity
- Desire to work closely with people
- Strong interest in improving the quality of home life
- Sensitivity to the practical needs of people
- Resourcefulness
- Dependability
- Organization
- Patience
- Tactfulness

Resources

- **American Dietetic Association**
  216 West Jackson Boulevard, Suite 800
  Chicago, IL 60606
  312-899-0040
  http://www.eatright.org/
  (offers information about scholarships, educational programs, and careers in dietetics)

- **National Child Care Association**
  1016 Rosser Street
  Conyers, GA 30012
  800-543-7161
  http://www.nccanet.org/
  (provides information regarding certification for child care professionals as well as a list of related organizations)

Horticulture

Horticulture is the branch of agriculture that involves the production and use of fruits, vegetables, and ornamental plants. It includes the study of trees, flowers, shrubs, vines, and grasses. Horticulture sites such as greenhouses, garden centers, and nurseries play an important role in the home gardening and landscaping pursuits of millions yearly. Specialties include fruits, vegetables, flowers, food handling, processing and storage, landscaping, arboriculture, turf and range management, nursery management, and plant breeding.

High School Courses

Science

Biology

Floral Arranging

Chemistry

Earth Science

Landscape Gardening

Gardening

Related Occupations

Agronomist—-B

Botanist—-B

Educator—-B/D

Florist—-V

Forester—-B

Horticulture Therapist—-B

Landscape Architect—-B

Nutritionist—-B

Plant Breeder—-B

Seed Analyst—-B

Soil Conservationist—-B

Tree Surgeon—-V

Biochemist—-B

Dietitian—-B

Entomologist—-B

Food Scientist—-B

Grounds Manager—-V

Horticulturist—-B

Landscape Gardener—-V

Park Ranger—-V

Plant Geneticist—-B/D

Silviculturist—-B

Technical Writer—-B

Leisure Activities

Working part-time in a garden center, nursery, fruit orchard, or greenhouse; reading publications related to horticulture; visiting botanical gardens, state and national parks, conservatories, and arboretums; attending flower shows and state fairs; gardening, canning, and freezing fruits and vegetables; developing hobbies and collections around flowers, leaves, house plants, or floral design; joining a science club, 4-H club, orchid club, or a conservation group; supporting or participating in natural resource preservation efforts; belonging to a professional organization such as the American Society for Horticultural Science; attending clinics, lectures, and workshops related to horticulture; working as a student aide in a high school or college greenhouse.

Skills

- A good understanding of and familiarity with plants of all types
- Physical stamina, good vision, and manual dexterity
- Ability to recognize differences in shapes, shading, and color
- Ability to work alone as well as with others
- Ability to make keen observations and sound judgments
- Proficiency in reading and writing
- General knowledge of horticulture supplies, equipment, services and business/marketing practices
- Proficiency for accuracy and detail
- Ability to manage and supervise others
- Ability to apply scientific methods to horticultural concerns

Values and Attributes

- Creativity
- Aesthetic awareness
- Desire to help humanity
- Independence
- A "green thumb"
- Strong interest in plants
- Fondness for outdoor activities
- Perseverance
- Industriousness
- Curiosity
- Imagination
- Cooperation
- Friendliness

Resources

- Garner, Jerry. *Careers in Horticulture and Botany.* VGM Career Horizons, 1997.
- **American Horticultural Therapy Association**
  362A Christopher Avenue
  Gaithersburg, MD 20879
  301-948-3010
  (encourages development of horticultural activities for therapeutic and rehabilitative purposes; offers student membership and job placement services)
- **American Society for Horticultural Science**
  60 Cameron Street
  Alexandria, VA 22314
  703-836-4606
  http://www.ashs.org/
  (offers career placement assistance and student membership, and sponsors college horticultural clubs)

Hotel/Motel Management

Hotel/motel management is concerned with the efficient profitable management and operation of hotels, motels, and other hospitality-oriented institutions. Study in this area focuses on customer service, public relations, marketing, sales, maintenance, housekeeping, supervision, hotel and restaurant management and service, sanitation and safety, budgeting, conventions, and personnel. Specializations include executive housekeeping, maintenance engineering, front office operations, food and beverage management, budget, sales, advertising, recreation, purchasing, accounting, personnel training, conventions, restaurant management, reservations, sanitation and safety, and security.

High School Courses

Business Management	Business
Math	Accounting
Foods	Food Service
Speech	Psychology
Economics	Sociology

Related Occupations

Airpost Manager—-B	Assistant Housekeeper—-V
Assistant Manager—-AA	Building Engineer—-AA/V
Building Manager—-V	Cafeteria Manager—-AA/V
Club Manager—-B	Director of Food and Beverage—-AA/V
Director of Sales—-B/V	Executive Housekeeper—-B
Food Production Manager—-V	Food Service Manager—-V
Front Office Manager—-V	General Manager—-B
Mall Manager—-B	Managing Director—-B
Marketing Manager—-B	Office Manager—-AA
Personnel Director—-B	Purchasing Agent—-B
Resident Manager—-B	YMCA/YWCA Director—-B

Leisure Activities

Working part-time as a bellhop, desk clerk, or hotel restaurant employee; organizing get-togethers, parties, or community events; leading a student group; participating on a debate or forensic team; participating in writing or oratory contests; reading publications related to management; attending lectures, workshops, and conferences related to hotel/motel management; joining a related professional organization; managing or helping others to manage apartments on a part-time basis.

Skills

- Proficiency in interpersonal communication
- Proficiency in reading, writing, and speaking
- Ability to solve problems and make appropriate decisions
- Ability to interact with people of different backgrounds and personalities
- Aptitude for accuracy and detail
- Ability to maintain composure under pressure and react spontaneously
- Good physical stamina, vision, and health
- Ability to accept public scrutiny and criticism
- Ability to supervise and coordinate the activities of others
- General knowledge of the hospitality industry
- Familiarity with business, finance, and marketing techniques
- Ability to persuade and influence others

Values and Attributes

- Recognition and appreciation from others
- Skill with people
- Achievement
- Desire to help others
- Willingness to "go the extra mile"
- Desire to work with and please others
- Willingness to work long and irregular hours and on weekends
- Pleasant and friendly personality
- Diplomacy
- Helpfulness
- Ability to adapt to frequent relocation
- Attentiveness
- Leadership
- Imagination
- Knowledge
- Energy

Resources

- Eberts, Marjorie, et al. *Careers in Travel, Tourism, and Hospitality.* VGM Career Horizons, 1997.
- *What Can I Do Now? Preparing for a Career in Travel and Hospitality.* Ferguson Publishing Company, 1998.
- **American Hotel and Motel Association**
  1201 New York Avenue, NW, Suite 600
  Washington, DC 20005
  202-289-3100
  http://www.ahma.com/
  (offers student membership and conducts training via home study, adult education, and college)
- **International Council on Hotel, Restaurant and Institutional Education**
  1200 17th Street, NW
  Washington, DC 20036
  202-331-5990
  (provides networking opportunities, publishes list of schools that offer training and education as well as the *Guide to Hospitality Education*)

Industrial Engineering

Industrial engineering study utilizes the principles and knowledge of science, mathematics, and engineering to efficiently and economically integrate people, machines, equipment, materials, and energy in order to maximize production and human benefit. Students are familiarized with techniques for efficient production, time-and-motion study, data processing design, management control, quality control, plant layout, safety procedures and conditions, and environment control. Specialties include operations research, management, ergonomics, environmental controls, plant layout and design, production planning and control, and computer processing.

High School Courses

Industrial Arts	Mechanical Drawing
Drafting	Blueprint Reading
Business Management	Economics
Math	Algebra
Geometry	Trigonometry
Calculus	Physical Science
Chemistry	

Related Occupations

Automotive Engineer—-B	Consulting Engineer—-B/M
Electrical Engineer—-B	Educator—-M/D
Environmental Engineer—-B	Fire Protection Engineer—-B
Human Resources Manager—-B	Industrial Engineer—-B
Manufacturing Engineer—-B	Materials Handling Engineer—-B
Mechanical Engineer—-B	Operations Engineer—-B
Plant Engineer—-B	Plastics Engineer—-B
Process Engineer—-B	Quality Control Engineer—-B
Research Engineer—-B/D	Safety Engineer—-B
Systems Analyst—-B	Systems Engineer—-B
Time Study Engineer—-B	

Leisure Activities

Participating in fundraising or social events that involve organization and planning; working part-time or as a volunteer in a supervisory position in a factory or a school industrial arts department; solving analytic, logic, and budgetary problems; reading publications related to engineering; attending engineering-related lectures and workshops; participating in clubs or organizations that require you to make oral presentations and write reports; working part-time as a research assistant.

Skills

- Ability to synthesize and integrate various factors of production
- Proficiency in mathematics and science
- Ability to make keen observations and sound judgments
- Proficiency in written and oral communication
- Ability to conduct and clearly communicate scientific research
- Knowledge of work measurements and standards
- Intellectual capacity to perform well in most undergraduate and graduate college programs
- Aptitude for leadership
- Ability to analyze, organize, and interpret scientific data
- Knowledge of basic manufacturing and assembly processes
- Good interpersonal skills and ability to work effectively with others

Values and Attributes

- Creativity
- Knowledge
- Achievement
- Desire to help others live better
- Enjoyment of challenges
- Interest in seeing ideas developed into practical use
- Initiative
- Perseverance
- Flexibility
- Organization
- Imagination
- Curiosity

Resources

- Camenson, Blythe. *Real People Working in Engineering*. VGM Career Horizons, 1998.
- **Institute of Industrial Engineers**
  25 Technology Park
  Norcross, GA 30092
  770-449-0460
  http://www.iienet.org/
  (provides information about educational opportunities and offers student membership)
- **Society of Women Engineers**
  120 Wall Street, 11th Floor
  New York, NY 10005
  http://wwwswe.org/
  (offers scholarship and career guidance information as well as a guide to assist women who want to be engineers)

Industrial and Precision Production/Technology

Industrial and precision production/technology is the study of the design and production of tools and machines as well as consumer products. This area is usually referred to as the machine trades field. Students are exposed to intricate and precise techniques of machine and product development. Areas of focus include blueprint reading, machine function and operation, precision and accuracy, applied mathematics, production, materials applications, installation, repair, and service. Specialties include tool-and-die, machines, job setting, toolmaking, machine operating, moldmaking, diemaking, inspection, instrument making, computer-aided design (CAD), and computer-aided manufacturing (CAM).

High School Courses

Industrial Arts	Mechanical Drawing
Blueprint Reading	Drafting
Machine/Metal Shop	Graphic Arts
Applied Math	Algebra
Geometry	Trigonometry

Related Occupations

Blacksmith—-V	Boilermaker—-V
Butcher—-V	Cabinetmaker—-V
CAD/CAM Operator—-V	Compositor—-V
Gunsmith—-V	Hand Molder—-V
Instrument Maker—-V	Jeweler—-V
Layout Worker—-V	Lithographer—-V
Locksmith—-V	Machine Operator—-V
Machine Repairer—-V	Machine Tool Operator—-V
Machinist—-V	Millwright—-V
Photoengraver—-V	Printing Press Operator—-V
Set Up Worker—-V	Shoe Repairer—-V
Tool and Die Maker—-V	Tool Programmer—-V
Upholsterer—-V	Welder—-V

Leisure Activities

Working part-time or as a volunteer worker in a machine shop, school industrial arts or metal shop; fixing and repairing mechanical items such as household appliances; overhauling car engines or building race cars, go-carts, dune buggies or other mechanical vehicles as a pasttime; reading mechanically related manuals and books; belonging to an organization such as the Vocational Industrial Clubs of America (VICA).

Skills

- Aptitude for mathematics and mechanics
- Aptitude for spatial perception, precision, accuracy, and detail
- Good vision, motor coordination, and manual and finger dexterity
- Knowledge of machine operations and industrial practices and trends
- Ability to read and interpret blueprints, diagrams, and schematic drawings
- Ability to follow directions and work alone as well as with others
- Ability to meet deadlines
- Thorough knowledge and ability in an area of specialization
- Ability to make sound judgments and appropriate decisions and solve problems
- Proficiency with computerized equipment

Values and Attributes

- Achievement
- Security
- Desire to be exact and to the point
- Ability to adapt to awkward and uncomfortable positions
- Enjoyment of hands-on activities
- Thoroughness
- Patience
- Precision
- Carefulness

Resources

- Basta, Nick. *Careers in High Tech: Second Edition.* VGM Career Horizons, 1999.
- Connelly, Robert. *Opportunities in Technical Education Programs.* VGM Career Horizons, 1998.
- *Exploring Tech Careers.* Ferguson Publishing Company, 1998.
- **Tooling and Manufacturing Association**
  1177 South Dee Road
  Park Ridge, IL 60068
  847-825-1120
  http://www.tmanet.com/
  (provides information about careers, school activities, and training programs)
- **National Tooling and Machining Association**
  9300 Livingston Road
  Fort Washington, MD 20744
  301-248-6200
  http://www.ntma.org/
  (promotes apprenticeship programs and conducts management training)

Law

Law is the study of the rules and guidelines by which a society maintains order and cooperation. The effective development, implementation, interpretation, and modification of rules and guidelines is a requirement for transmitting societal values and expectations. Study in law exposes the student to civil and constitutional law, contracts, property, legal methods, research and writing, torts, criminal law and taxation, lawyer and client theory, law history, and many other areas. Specialties include civil, criminal, or labor; real estate, corporate, or patent; tort, international, or taxation; entertainment, trust, or admiralty; bankruptcy; and environmental law.

High School Courses

Civics

Public Speaking

Debate

English

Sociology

Government

Speech

Forensics

Psychology

Related Occupations

Adjudicator—-P

Appeals Referee—-P

Bankruptcy Attorney—-P

Corporation Lawyer—-P

District Attorney—-P

Employment Lawyer—-P

Escrow Officer—-B

Judge—-P

Parole/Probation Officer—-B

Patent Lawyer—-P

Tax Attorney—-P

Traffic Court Magistrate—-P

Admiralty Lawyer—-D

Appellate Court Judge—-P

Bar Examiner—-P

Criminal Lawyer—-P

District Court Judge—-P

Environmental Lawyer—-P

Insurance Attorney—-P

Lawyer—-P

Patent Agent—-B

Real Estate Buyer—-B

Title Attorney—-P

Trial Court Judge—-P

Leisure Activities

Participating in activities that involve research; visiting libraries and attending court sessions; reading law publications; viewing dramas or documentaries on TV or at a theater; attending lectures or conferences related to law; working part-time or as a volunteer in a law office or department; joining a student government or newspaper staff; freelance or technical writing; participating in a community association; joining a debate or forensics team; competing in oratory contests; conversing with others.

Skills

- Ability to speak articulately, read comprehensively, and write well
- Ability to persuade and influence others
- Broad background of general knowledge
- Ability to make keen observations and sound judgments
- Ability to research, collect, organize, and clearly present information to others
- Familiarity with legal practices, policies, and trends
- Intellectual capacity to perform well in most undergraduate and graduate programs
- Ability to analyze and evaluate data, make appropriate decisions and solve problems
- Ability to communicate abstract ideas to others
- Aptitude for accuracy and detail
- Aptitude for leadership

Values and Attributes

- Intellectual growth
- Power
- Prestige
- Desire for recognition and appreciation from others
- Ability to work under pressure, meet deadlines, and accept close public scrutiny and criticism
- High regard for and appreciation of the law and an orderly society
- Sensitivity to the needs of human beings
- Persistence
- Integrity
- Resourcefulness
- Persuasiveness
- Analytical mind
- Trustworthiness

Resources

- Smith, Janet. *Beyond L.A. Law: Inspiring Stories of People Who've Done Fascinating Things with a Law Degree.* Harcourt Brace Legal Division, 1998.
- *So You Want to Be a Lawyer: A Practical Guide to Law as a Career.* Broadway Books, 1998.
- **American Bar Association**
  750 North Lake Shore Drive
  Chicago, IL 60611
  312-988-5000
  http://www.abanet.org/
  (provides information about bar exam preparation, student membership, scholarships, law schools, and career publications)
- **Law School Admission Council**
  PO Box 40
  Newtown, PA 18940
  25-968-1001
  http://www.lsac.org/
  (offers *Frequently Asked Questions, Choosing a Law School,* and financial aid information)

Legal and Protective Services

Legal and protective services is the study of several related fields which focus on the effective implementation of law and legal procedures as well as the relationship of laws to the safety and protection of life and property. Legal services involves research and support related to the understanding and interpretation of law, legal procedures, and practices. Study in protective services concentrates on the implementation of laws aimed at ensuring the peaceful cooperation, security, and safety of human lives and property. Some specialties are legal assisting, criminal justice and public safety, corrections and rehabilitation, and law enforcement.

High School Courses

Civics

Government

ROTC

Psychology

Social Studies

Sociology

Physical Education

Health

Related Occupations

Administrative Examiner—-P

Bailiff—-V

Border Patrol Officer—-AA

Case Worker—-B

Corrections Officer—-AA

Criminal Investigator—-AA

Deputy Sheriff—-AA

Detective—-AA

District Attorney—-P

Drug Enforcement Officer—-AA

Firefighter—-AA

Fish and Game Warden—-AA/B

Guard—-V

Lifeguard—-V/AA

Military Officer—-B

Paralegal—-AA/B

Parole/Probation Officer—-B

Penologist—-B

Police Commissioner—-B

Police Officer—-AA

Polygraph Examiner—-AA/B

Private Investigator—-V

Public Safety Captain—-AA

Security Officer—-V

Social Service Worker—-V

Special Agent—-B

Warden (Prison)—-B

Leisure Activities

Working part-time or as a volunteer in a fire or police station, law office, or marketing research firm; participating in activities that involve investigation and research; viewing law-related dramas and documentaries on TV; visiting libraries; reading publications related to legal or protective services; working as a security guard; writing reports; participating in student government; belonging to a debate or forensics team; serving in the armed forces.

Skills

- Background of legal knowledge
- Ability to react spontaneously and maintain composure under pressure
- Proficiency in reading, writing, and speaking
- Ability to make appropriate decisions and sound judgments
- Ability to interact with people of different personalities and backgrounds
- Ability to solve problems and meet deadlines
- Proficiency in interpersonal communication
- Aptitude for accuracy and detail
- Ability to persuade and influence others
- Ability to conduct and clearly explain scientific research
- Good vision, health, physical stamina, and manual dexterity

Values and Attributes

- Security
- Wisdom
- Desire to help others
- Appreciation for order and thoroughness
- Tendency toward analytical and logical thinking
- Interest in investigating and exploring for factual detail
- Integrity
- Persistence
- Alertness
- Trustworthiness
- Desire for challenges

Resources

- Hutton, Donald and Anna Mydlarz. *Guide to Law Enforcement Careers.* Barron's, 1997.
- Lee, Mary, et al. *100 Best Careers in Crime Fighting: Law Enforcement, Criminal Justice, Private Security, and Cyberspace Crime Detection.* Arco, 1998.
- *What Can I Do Now? Preparing for a Career in Public Safety.* Ferguson Publishing Company, 1998.
- **American Correctional Association**
  4380 Forbes Boulevard
  Lanham, MD 20706
  800-222-5646
  http://www.corrections.com/aca/
  (provides a job bank and information about standards and accreditation)
- **American Jail Association**
  2053 Day Road, Suite 100
  Hagertstown, MS 21740
  301-790-3930
  http://www.corrections.com/aja/
  (offers list of college programs and provides job search assistance)

Library and Information Sciences

Library and information sciences is the study of how information of all kinds is stored, organized, classified, and made available for use by others. Study in this area exposes students to the intricate logistics required for acquiring, circulating, and maintaining massive amounts of informational materials for those who want and need it. Students also learn various ways to access information as well as techniques of promotion. Major concentrations within this field are many and include materials for children and young adults, reference materials, audiovisual, school and college services, special library services, cataloging, special collections, material acquisitions, adult materials, community outreach, information systems, and administration.

High School Courses

English	Language Arts
Speed Reading	Social Studies
Anthropology	Literature
World	History
Management	Sociology

Related Occupations

Academic Librarian—-M	Acquisitions Librarian—-M
Archivist—-M	Bibliographer—-M
Book Conservator—-M	Cataloger—-M
Children's Librarian—-M	Classifier—-M
Community Outreach Librarian—-M	Information Scientist—-M/D
Librarian—-M	Library Assistant—-V
Library Consultant—-M/D	Library Director—-M/D
Library Technician—-C/AA	Media Center Manager—-M Medical
Public Librarian—-M	Reference Librarian—-M
Special Collections Librarian—-M	Systems Analyst—-M

Leisure Activities

Reading; freelance writing; attending book fairs, used book sales, and book stores; visiting libraries and museums; belonging to a book club, literary society, or professional organization such as the American Library Association; attending lectures, workshops, and conferences related to library and information sciences; working part-time or as a volunteer in a library, bookstore, law office, or research firm; participating in activities that involve research; subscribing to a professional publication; collecting items such as stamps or rare books.

Skills

- Knowledge in an area of specialization as well as a background of general knowledge
- Proficiency in reading and grammar and an extensive vocabulary
- Ability to organize, collect, classify, arrange, and coordinate materials of all kinds
- Ability to critically evaluate, make sound judgments, and appropriate decisions, and solve problems
- Good vision and physical stamina
- Proficiency in interpersonal communication
- Ability to work with others as well as work quietly alone for long periods of time
- Ability to conduct and clearly explain scientific research
- Intellectual ability to perform well in most undergraduate and graduate college programs
- Aptitude for accuracy, detail, and memorization
- Proficiency with computers

Values and Attributes

- Intellectual growth
- Wisdom
- Desire to help others learn
- Love of reading and exploring for information
- Willingness to engage in lifelong learning
- Flexibility
- Resourcefulness
- Analytical mind
- Intellectual curiosity
- Perseverance
- Alertness

Resources

- McCook, Kathleen de la Pena. *Opportunities in Library and Information Science Careers*. VGM Career Horizons, 1997.
- **American Library Association**
  50 East Huron Street
  Chicago, IL 60611
  800-545-2433
  http://www.ala.org/
  (provides employment and scholarship information as well as career-related publications)
- **Special Libraries Association**
  1700 Eighteenth Street, NW
  Washington, DC 20009
  202-234-4700
  http://www.sla.org/
  (offers *What's a Special Librarian?*, competencies for special librarians, and career and employment tips)

Marketing and Distribution

Marketing and distribution is a major field in the area of business which involves the study of consumer needs and desires for products and services, consumers' willingness and ability to pay for these needs/desires, and the geographical vicinity in which they reside. A large focus is on the various strategies used to attract and motivate people to buy or subscribe to a product or service and the numerous methods of distribution. Specializations in this area include sales, advertising, sales promotion, retail, brand management, and marketing research.

High School Courses

Business

Advertising

Fashion Merchandising

Speech

Forensics

Sales

Economics

Psychology

Debate

Related Occupations

Advertising Account Executive—-B

Advertising Salesperson—-AA

Buyer—-B

Director of Marketing—-V

Fashion Model—-V

Human Resources Manager—-B/M

Manufacturer Sales Workers—-AA

Merchandise Manager—-B

Package Designer—-B

Product Manager—-B

Real Estate Agent—-AA

Sales Promotion Manager—-B

Securities Sales Agent—-B

Store Controller—-B

Wireless Sales Worker—-V

Advertising Manager—-B

Assistant Buyer—-B

Direct Salesperson—-AA

Economist—-B

Field Representative—-AA

Insurance Agent—-B/V

Market Research Analyst—-B

Online Marketer—-V/B

Pharmaceutical Sales Representative—-B

Purchasing Agent—-B

Sales Manager—-B

Sales Supervisor—-B

Sports/Special Events Executive—-B/M

Store Manager—-B

Leisure Activities

Working part-time in a department store, advertising firm, warehouse, or wholesale/retail establishment; belonging to a Junior Achievement Club, Distributive Education Club (DECA), or professional organization such as the American Marketing Association; participating in oratory contests; participating on a debate or forensics team; attending auctions, political rallies, or sales lectures; participating in a civic fundraising event or in student government; writing promotional materials; reading publications related to marketing and distribution; attending sales and marketing workshops and conferences; serving as a student aide in a school or college distributive education or marketing department; selling products or services on a part-time basis.

Skills

- Ability to work well with people of different personalities and backgrounds
- Ability to make appropriate decisions and sound judgments
- Ability to persuade and influence others
- A good vocabulary
- Articulateness
- Good knowledge of marketing techniques and consumer products and needs
- Ability to solve problems
- Physical stamina and emotional well-being
- Ability to conduct and apply the results of consumer research
- Aptitude for selling

Values and Attributes

- Achievement
- Prestige
- Wealth
- Desire for recognition and appreciation from others
- Creativity
- Outgoing, polite, and friendly attitude
- Desire to serve and please others
- Tendency to be alert and ambitious
- Competitiveness and flexibility
- Energy
- Patience
- Poise
- Neatness
- Self-confidence

RELATED Resources

- Steinberg, Margery. *Opportunities in Marketing Careers.* VGM Career Horizons, 1999.
- **American Marketing Association**
  250 South Wacker Drive
  Chicago, IL 60606
  312-648-0536
  http://www.ama.org/
  (provides a career bibliography and a brochure entitled, *Invest in Your Future,* invites student membership, and publishes a student newsletter)
- **Sales and Marketing Executives International**
  5500 Interstate Nunta Parkway, Suite 545
  Atlanta, GA 30328
  770-661-8500
  http://smei.org/
  (offers *What is Professional Certification?* and a pop quiz on the Internet to determine suitability for this type of profession)

Mathematics

Mathematics is the study of quantitative relationships expressed in numbers and symbols. It focuses on mathematical concepts and theories and involves their formulation, testing, interpretation, and practical application. Mathematics is usually referred to as either pure (more theoretical and abstract) or applied (more practical and result-oriented). Mathematics in some form or manner is used by just about everyone. A minimal understanding and use of mathematics is considered basic to daily life. Major branches include arithmetic, algebra, geometry, trigonometry, calculus, probability, and statistics.

High School Courses

Math	Algebra
Geometry	Trigonometry
Calculus	Statistics
Accounting	Physics

Related Occupations

Accountant—-B	Actuary—-B/M
Aerospace Engineer—-B	Appraiser—-B
Astronomer—-D	Bank Officer—-AA/B
Bookkeeper—-AA	Cartographer—-B
Computer Programmer—-B	Credit Manager—-AA/B
Educator—-B/D	Financial Planner—-B
Market Research Analyst—-B	Mathematician—-B/D
Nuclear Scientist—-B/D	Physicist—-B/D
Radar Technician—-AA	Statistician—-B
Surveyor—-AA	Systems Analyst—-B
Tool and Die Maker—-V	

Leisure Activities

Doing jigsaw puzzles and playing games of strategy; participating in tournaments, quiz bowls, and other competitive events; solving problems involving analytical and logical processes; joining a math club, science organization, or investment group; serving as a committee or church treasurer or as a financial officer for a civic or social agency; working as a part-time or volunteer sports statistician; reading math or science publications.

Skills

- Ability to make sound judgments and decisions and to solve quantitative problems
- Ability to concentrate for long periods of time
- Proficiency in writing, speaking, and memorization
- Proficiency for accuracy and detail
- Ability to understand both concrete and abstract mathematical concepts
- Ability to organize, analyze, and interpret numerical data
- Ability to make keen observations
- Ability to conduct and clearly explain scientific research
- Proficiency in use of scientific calculator

Values and Attributes

- Independence
- Intellectual growth
- Achievement
- Security
- Ability to frame inquiry and respond objectively
- Tendency toward analytical and logical thinking
- Capacity for precision and detail
- Desire for challenges
- Thoroughness
- Imagination
- Patience
- Persistence
- Self-discipline

Resources

- Lambert, Stephen and Ruth DeCotis. *Great Jobs for Math Majors.* VGM Career Horizons, 1999.
- **American Mathematical Society**
  PO Box 5904
  Boston, MA 02206-5904
  800-321-4267
  http://www.ams.org/
  (helps those seeking employment, assistantships, and graduate fellowships; publishes a brochure entitled *Careers in Mathematics*)
- **American Statistical Association**
  1429 Duke Street
  Alexandria, VA 22314
  703-684-1221
  http://www.amstat.org/
  (Offers free of charge: *Careers in Statistics, Women in Statistics,* and *Minorities— Looking for a Challenging Career? What about Statistics?*)
- **Mathematical Association of America**
  PO Box 90973
  Washington, DC 20090
  800-331-1622
  http://www.maa.org/
  (offers *Careers in the Mathematical Sciences, More Careers in the Mathematical Sciences,* and *Mathematical Scientists at Work*)

Mechanical Engineering

Mechanical engineering focuses on the practical application of science, mathematics, and energy in the design and development of machines and related mechanical equipment that produce and use power as well as those used in manufacturing products. Internal combustion engines, motors of all types, nuclear reactors, refrigerators, elevators, robots, and a variety of medical equipment are some of the visible results of mechanical engineering. Specialties in this field include automotive, air-conditioning/refrigeration and heating, research, nuclear power, and aircraft.

High School Courses

Math	Algebra
Geometry	Trigonometry
Calculus	Mechanical Drawing
Blueprint Reading	Industrial Arts
Mechanics	Small Engine Repair
Physical Science	Physics

Related Occupations

Aerospace Engineer—-B/D	Astronaut—-B
Automotive Engineer—-B	Biomedical Engineer—-B
Computer Science Engineer—-B	Consulting Engineer—-B/M
Electrical Engineer—-B	Engineer—-B
Engineering Mechanic—-AA	Engineering Technician—-AA
Heating and Air-conditioning Engineer—-B	
Industrial Engineer—-B	Materials Handling Engineer—-B
Mechanical Drafter—-AA	Mechanical Engineer—-B
Mechanical Engineering Technician—-AA	
Millwright—-V	Packaging Engineer—-B
Plastics Engineer—-B	Research Engineer—-B/D
Safety Engineer—-B	Systems Analyst—-B
Systems Engineer—-B	Test Engineer—-B

Leisure Activities

Tinkering with electrical appliances or other mechanical devices; participating in a club or organization that requires you to make oral presentations and write reports; developing hobbies related to radios, stereos, building go-carts, fixing cars, and other similar activities; reading publications related to mechanics or engineering; belonging to a student or professional engineering organization; working part-time or as a volunteer in an engineering firm, mechanic shop, or engineering department; attending lectures and workshops and taking leisure classes related to mechanical engineering.

Skills

- Ability to make keen observations and sound judgments
- Proficiency in mathematics and science
- Ability to synthesize and integrate various factors of production
- Proficiency in written and oral communication
- Ability to conduct and clearly communicate scientific research
- Intellectual capacity to perform well in most undergraduate and graduate college programs
- Ability to work well with others
- Ability to solve problems and make appropriate decisions
- Aptitude for accuracy and detail, spatial perception, and abstract reasoning
- Manual dexterity and understanding of mechanics
- Proficiency with computers
- Proficiency in an area of specialization and knowledge of current practices and trends
- Sensitivity to economic considerations and human needs

Values and Attributes

- Creativity
- Achievement
- Knowledge
- Desire to help others live better
- Interest in seeing ideas developed into practical use
- Desire for challenges
- Imagination
- Flexibility
- Persuasiveness
- Curiosity
- Thoroughness
- Responsibility

Resources

- Camenson, Blythe. *Real People Working in Engineering.* VGM Career Horizons, 1998.
- **American Society of Heating, Refrigerating and Air-Conditioning Engineers**
  1791 Tullie Circle, NE
  Atlanta, GA 30329
  404-636-8400
  http://www.ashrae.org/
- **American Society of Mechanical Engineers**
  22 Law Drive, Box 2900
  Fairfield, NJ 07007
  800-843-2763
  http://www.asme.org/
  (publishes information about mechanical engineering careers and financial aid)

Mechanics and Related Services

Mechanics involves the study of machine design, building, operation, repair, and service. Mechanics covers a broad range and include appliances, communication and computer equipment, industrial machinery, and office machines as well as vehicle and mobile mechanics. Among the specialties within this area are automotive, aircraft, diesel, farm equipment, appliances, office machines, radio/TV, air-conditioning, refrigeration, and heating.

High School Courses

Automotive Mechanics	Small Engine Repair
Mechanical Drawing	Applied Math
Algebra	Electronics

Related Occupations

Air-conditioning, Refrigeration, and Heating Mechanic—-AA

Aircraft Mechanic—-AA	Automotive Body Repairer—-V
Automotive Mechanic—-V	Bicycle Repairer—-V
Cable Splicer—-V	

Commercial/Industrial Electronic Equipment Repairer—-V

Computer Service Technician—-AA	Diesel Mechanic—-V

Electronic Home Equipment Repairer—-V

Engine Specialist—-V	Farm Equipment Mechanic—-V
General Maintenance Mechanic—-V	Gunsmith—-V
Industrial Machine Repairer—-V	Instrument Mechanic—-V
Instrument Repairer—-V	Instrumentation Technician—-AA/V
Line Installer—-V	Locksmith—-V
Millwright—-V	Motorcycle Mechanic—-V
Musical Instrument Repairer—-V	Office Machine Servicer—-V
Telephone Installer/ Repairer—-V	Vending Machine Servicer—-V
Watchmaker—-V	

Leisure Activities

Working part-time or as a volunteer mechanic in a service station or bicycle repair or small engine shop; repairing electric appliances or other mechanical gadgetry; reading manuals and books related to auto mechanics; developing hobbies and collections related to cars, model kits, or racing; doing your own car repair; building and/or repairing go-carts, mini-bikes, lawn mowers, or scooters; auto shows; racing.

Skills

- Good health, vision, hearing, and coordination
- Aptitude for mechanics
- Ability to read and understand technical and service manuals and diagrams
- Good listening skills
- Able to work alone as well as with others
- Ability to meet deadlines
- Ability to interact with people with different personalities and backgrounds
- Proficiency in spatial perception and mechanical dexterity
- Ability to make sound judgments and appropriate decisions and solve problems
- Proficiency in an area of mechanical specialization

Values and Attributes

- Skill
- Accomplishment
- Security
- Willingness to work with dirty, greasy materials and sometimes in awkward and hazardous positions
- Enjoyment of hands-on activities
- Willingness to continue training and education throughout life
- Dependability
- Precision
- Trustworthiness
- Carefulness
- Thoroughness

Resources

- Weber, Robert. *Opportunities in Automotive Service Careers.* VGM Career Horizons, 1997.
- **National Institute for Automotive Service Excellence**
  1305 Dulles Technology Drive, Suite 2
  Herndon, VA 20171
  703-713-3800
  http://www.asecert.org/
  (publishes *ASE Blue Seal Tech News* as well as preparation guides and sample test questions; promotes high standards of automotive service)
- **Professional Aviation Maintenance Association**
  636 I Street, NW, Suite 300
  Washington, DC 20001
  202-216-9220
  http://www.pama.org/
  (offers scholarships and publishes *Your Career in Aviation Maintenance*)
- **Vocational Industrial Clubs of America**
  PO Box 3000
  Leesburg, VA 20177
  703-777-8810
  http://www.vica.org/
  (promotes high standards of workmanship and provides students with information on educational, job, and personal development skills)

Medicine

Medicine is a branch of the health sciences and focuses on the application of medicine and medical techniques in the treatment, care, and prevention of disease, illness, and injury in both humans and animals. Students of medicine are exposed to how medical knowledge and procedures, drugs, and technology assist to minimize pain and preserve the health of millions. Among the numerous specialties are anesthesiology, colon and rectal surgery, dermatology, family practice, internal medicine, neurology, obstetrics and gynecology, pediatrics, urology, gastroenterology, surgery, dentistry, psychiatry, and veterinary medicine.

High School Courses

Health	Science
Biology	Chemistry
Physiology	First Aid
Physical Education	Algebra
Geometry	Trigonometry

Related Occupations

Allergist—-P	Anesthesiologist—-P
Cardiologist—-P	Chiropractor—-P
Dentist—-P	Dermatologist—-P
Endocrinologist—-P	Gastroenterologist—-P
Geriatrician—-P	Gynecologist—-P
Immunologist—-P	Internist—-P
Neurologist—-P	Obstetrician—-P
Ophthalmologist—-P	Optometrist—-P
Orthodontist—-P	Osteopath—-P
Pathologist—-P	Pediatrician—-P
Pharmacologist—-P	Physician—-P
Physician Assistant—-B	Plastic Surgeon—-P
Podiatrist—-P	Psychiatrist—-P
Radiologist—-P	Reproductive Endocrinologist—-P
Surgeon—-P	Urologist—-P
Veterinarian—-P	

Leisure Activities

Attending medical science fairs and exhibits and visiting science museums; reading medically related publications; joining a health club; doing lab experiments and researching medically related topics; belonging to a medical science club or related professional organization; working as a part-time or volunteer in a local hospital, nursing home, or community health agency; actively participating in or financially supporting medical research efforts; attending lectures and conferences related to medicine.

Skills

- High proficiency for accuracy and detail
- Ability to react quickly and maintain emotional and physical composure in stressful situations
- Proficiency in interpersonal communication
- Ability to work well and concentrate under pressure
- Proficiency in critical thinking, analyzing, and problem-solving
- Physical stamina, good vision, and manual dexterity
- Intellectual capacity to perform well in most undergraduate and graduate college programs
- Thorough knowledge of medical theories and practices
- Ability to conduct and clearly explain scientific research
- Ability to make keen observations and appropriate decisions
- Aptitude for applied science
- Proficiency in reading and memorization

Values and Attributes

- Prestige
- Health
- Wisdom
- Achievement
- Desire to help others and make a contribution to humanity
- Interest in challenges
- Willingness to work long and irregular hours
- Desire to alleviate the pain and suffering of others
- Scientific inquiry
- Analytical mind
- Perseverance
- Dedication
- Imagination
- Alertness

Resources

- Danek, Marita and Jennifer. *Becoming a Physician*. 1997.
- Gable, Fred. *Opportunities in Pharmacy Careers*. VGM Career Horizons, 1998.
- **American Medical Association**
  515 North State Street
  Chicago, IL 60610
  312-464-5000
  http://www.ama.assn.org/
  (offers membership and job placement services and publishes numerous periodicals)
- **American Optometric Association**
  243 North Lindbergh Boulevard
  St. Louis, MO 63141
  314-999-4100
  http://www.aoanet.org/
  (publishes *What Is a Doctor of Optometry?* and provides an informative career guidance section on the Internet)
- **American Osteopathic Association**
  142 East Ontario Street
  Chicago, IL 60611
  312-280-5800
  (provides scholarships, placement services, and information about schools and licensure)

Metallurgical and Mining Engineering

Metallurgical and mining engineering is the practical application of science, mathematics, and energy in the extraction, treatment, and processing of metals, coal, and other nonmetallic resources from the earth. It involves the research and refinement of these natural materials along with the development of processes to enable the production and discovery of products necessary to the success and comfort of an industrialized society. Students may elect to concentrate in research, extractive engineering, processing, applications, management, or other areas.

High School Courses

Math	Algebra
Geometry	Trigonometry
Calculus	Science
Physical Science	Earth Science
Chemistry	Mechanical Drawing
Blueprint Reading	Industrial Arts

Related Occupations

Ceramic Engineer—-B	Chemical Engineer—-B
Civil Engineer—-B	Construction Engineer—-B
Consulting Engineer—-B/M	Electrical Engineer—-B
Environmental Engineer—-B	Geological Engineer—-B
Geologist—-B	Geophysical Engineer—-B
Geophysicist—-B	Materials Handling Engineer—-B
Metallurgical Engineer—-B	Metallurgical Engineering Technician—-AA
Metallurgist—-B	Mining Engineer—-B
Nuclear Engineer—-B	Petroleum Engineer—-B
Pipeline Engineer—-B	Plastics Engineer—-B
Research Engineer—-B	Safety Engineer—-B
Sanitary Engineer—-B	Systems Engineer—-B

Leisure Activities

Developing hobbies and interests related to building items out of metal or other materials, rock and mineral collections, and mechanics; reading publications about engineering or metallurgical topics; attending related lectures and workshops; doing experiments to see how materials react; working part-time with a mining company, in a foundry, or in a college engineering department; belonging to a student or professional engineering organization; solving analytic and logic problems; participating in clubs or organizations that require you to make oral presentations and write reports.

Skills

- Ability to analyze, organize, and interpret scientific data
- Ability to work well with others
- Ability to make appropriate decisions and solve problems
- Ability to make keen observations and sound judgments
- Aptitude for accuracy and detail, spatial perception, and abstract reasoning
- Sensitivity to economic considerations and human needs
- Proficiency in an area of specialization and knowledgeable of current practices and trends
- Proficiency in written and oral communication
- Ability to conduct and clearly communicate scientific research
- Intellectual capacity to perform well in most undergraduate and graduate college programs
- Proficiency with computers

Values and Attributes

- Creativity
- Achievement
- Desire to help others live better
- Desire for challenges
- Interest in seeing ideas developed into practical use
- Curiosity
- Imagination
- Perseverance
- Flexibility
- Alertness

Resources

- Camenson, Blythe. *Real People Working in Engineering.* VGM Career Horizons, 1998.
- **ASM International**
  9639 Kinsman Road
  Materials Park, OH 44073
  440-338-5151
  http://www.asm-intl.org/
  (distributes information about the manufacture, use, and treatment of engineered materials and conducts a career development program)
- **Mineral Information Institute**
  475 17th Street, No. 510
  Denver, CO 80202
  303-297-3226
  http://www.mii.org/
  (publishes *Opportunities for a Career in Mining, Metallurgy, and Materials*)

Military Science

Military science is the study of the philosophies, theories, and practices of military leadership and warfare. Effective implementation of the principles of military science is considered vital to the protection of a country's citizens. Military science exposes students to military history, the nature of war, leadership and management skills, organization, customs and traditions, first aid, lifesaving and survival techniques, weaponry, marksmanship, equipment use and design, methods of combat, offensive and defensive strategies, and communications. The five major concentrations within military science are communications, engineering, logistics, strategy, and tactics. Keep in mind that some of the occupations cited below are limited to simulated or actual war environments. However, many of the skills developed in preparation for them (particularly leadership, administration, and management skills) are transferable to civilian occupations such as engineering, clerical, maintenance, and mechanics.

High School Courses

ROTC	Physical Education
Civics	Government
Law	Social Studies
Sociology	Psychology
History	World History

Related Occupations

Administrative Officer—-B	Airplane Engineer—-B/V
Airplane Pilot—-B/V	Air Traffic Controller—-V
Career Counselor—-B/M	Cartographer—-AA/V
Computer Programmer—-AA	Diver—-V
Educator—-B/M	Electronic Technician—-AA/V
Engineering Officer—-B	Graphic Designer—-AA
Human Rights Counselor—-B/M	Intelligence Specialist—-B/D
Interpreter/Translator—-B	Journalist—-AA/B
Medical Laboratory Technician—-AA	Musician—-B/V
Public Information Specialist—-AA/B	Radio Equipment Technician—-AA/V
Recruiter—-AA/B	ROTC Instructor—-B
Ship's Pilot—-B	Systems Analyst—-B
Topographic Engineer—-B	Trainer—-AA/B

Leisure Activities

Participating in an ROTC program; belonging to a national guard unit; playing games of logic, strategy, and warfare; serving in a branch of the armed forces; reading publications related to the military; attending military-related lectures and conferences; viewing war-related TV programs and movies; working part-time or as a volunteer in a police station or as a security guard; visiting military exhibits; participating in competitive team and individual sports.

Skills

- Intellectual capacity to do well in most undergraduate and graduate programs
- Aptitude for leadership
- Proficiency for analytical and logical reasoning
- Ability to react instantly and maintain composure in stressful situations
- Proficiency in reading and understanding directions
- Ability to make sound judgments and appropriate decisions
- Ability to interact with people of different personalities and backgrounds
- Good vision and health
- Physical stamina, good motor coordination, and manual dexterity
- Ability to clearly communicate ideas and concepts to others
- Ability to motivate and extract loyalty from others
- Background in military history, principles, and procedures

Values and Attributes

- Loyalty
- Independence
- Security
- Achievement
- Willingness to follow orders and take risks
- Courage
- Ability to respond well in emergencies
- Order and discipline
- Perseverance
- Analytical mind
- Competitive drive
- Spontaneity
- Responsibility
- Determination

Resources

- Hutton, Donald. *Guide to Military Careers*. Barron's, 1998.
- Paradis, Adrian. *Opportunities in Military Careers*. VGM Career Horizons, 1999.
- **Association of Military Colleges and Schools of the United States**
  9429 Garden Court
  Potomac, MD 20834
  301-765-0695
- In addition, contact the area recruiting office of the military branch you are interested in (see "Recruiting" in the Yellow Pages). The Army, Air Force, Navy, Marine Corps, and Coast Guard can all be called toll-free.

Nursing and Related Services

Nursing and related services is the study of the direct personal care, support, and condition monitoring (usually accompanied by frequent hands-on activities) of those who are sick, injured, handicapped, or elderly. Students learn about the day-to-day skills and practices involved in quality patient care. Study includes learning about human anatomical and physiological processes, human growth, development, and behavior as well as teamwork, observation, and referral, responding to emergencies, health care facility operations, philosophy and management, and diet and nutrition. Some of the specialties under nursing and related services are midwifery, occupational nursing, public health nursing, physical therapy, occupational therapy, school nursing, private duty nursing, and recreational therapy.

High School Courses

Health	Science
Biology	Chemistry
Physiology	Applied Math
Algebra	Geometry
First Aid	

Related Occupations

Art Therapist—-B	Athletic Trainer—-B
General Duty Nurse—-AA/B	Head Nurse—-B/M
Licensed Practical Nurse—-C	Music Therapist—-B
Nurse Anesthetist—-M	Nurse Clinician—-M
Nurse Instructor—-B	Nurse-Midwife—-M
Nurse Practitioner—-M	Nurse Supervisor—-B
Occupational Therapist—-B	Physical Therapist—-B
Private Duty Nurse—-AA/B	Recreational Therapist—-B
Registered Nurse—-AA/B	Respiratory Therapist—-AA
School Nurse—-B	

Leisure Activities

Attending lectures, workshops, and conferences related to nursing; belonging to a health guild, club, or advisory board; watching TV programs or movies related to hospitals, nursing, or medicine; reading nursing-related publications; belonging to a professional organization such as the National League of Nursing (NLN); working part-time or as a volunteer in a hospital, nursing home, health agency, or college nursing department; actively supporting health care and charitable efforts.

Skills

- Aptitude for applied science
- Ability to make keen observations, sound judgments, and appropriate decisions
- Thorough knowledge of nursing and/or related practices and techniques
- Proficiency for accuracy and detail
- Physical stamina, good vision, and manual dexterity
- Ability to solve problems
- Proficiency in reading, writing, and following directions
- Understanding of normal human behavior, growth, and development
- Ability to react spontaneously and maintain emotional and physical composure in stressful situations
- Ability to work cooperatively with people of different backgrounds and personalities

Values and Attributes

- Health
- Wisdom
- Desire to work directly with people and to help others
- Warm, understanding, and friendly attitude
- Sensitivity to the needs and pain of others
- Willingness to work irregular hours and on weekends
- Patience
- Self-confidence
- Poise
- Responsibility
- Capability

Resources

- Case, Bette. Ph.D., R.N. *Career Planning for Nurses.* Delmar, 1997.
- Eagles, Zardoya, R.N. *The Nurses Career Guide: Discovering New Horizons in Health Care.* Sovereignty Press, 1997.
- Katz, Janet. *Majoring in Nursing: From Prerequisites to Postgraduate Study and Beyond.* Noonday Press, 1999.
- *What Can I Do Now? Preparing for a Career in Nursing.* Ferguson Publishing Company, 1998.
- **American Nurses Association**
  600 Maryland Avenue, SW
  Suite 100 West
  Washington, DC 20024
  202-651-7000
  http://www.nursingworld.org/
  (offers *Voices from the Past, Visions of the Future*)
- **National Student Nurses Association**
  555 West 57th Street, Suite 1327
  New York, NY 10019
  212-581-2211
  http://www.nsna.org/
  (offers scholarships, assistance for state boards, and prep materials for state license exams)

Performing Arts

Study in the performing arts offers exposure to creative dramatic expression, primarily in front of live audiences. It involves study of all types of artistic performance in theaters, in educational institutions, on TV, in movies, and outdoors. All major aspects of performance preparation are studied. These include set design, stage setup, scenery, decorations, light and sound production, costumes, and makeup. Speaking techniques and developing stage presence are also taught. Major specializations include acting, singing, comedy, and dance.

High School Courses

Drama	Theater
Arts	Debate
Forensics	Dance
Band	Orchestra
Choir	Public Speaking
Speech	Physical Education

Related Occupations

Actor/Actress—-AA/B	Announcer (Radio, TV)—-AA/B
Choreographer—-B	Circus Performer—-V
Comedian—-V	Composer—-B
Costumer—-V	Dancer—-V
Dance Instructor—-B/V	Drama Coach—-B/M
Educator—-B/D	Fashion Model—-V
Film Director—-B	Magician—-V
Merchandise Displayer—-AA	Motion Picture Photographer—-B
Musician—-B	Music Director—-B
Music Teacher—-B/M	Orchestra Conductor—-B/V
Producer—B	Public Relations Specialist—-B
Puppeteer—-V	Set Designer—-B
Singer—-B	Stage Manager—-B

Leisure Activities

Participating in local theater productions; attending plays, concerts, lectures, and movies; working part-time or as a volunteer for a radio or TV station; joining a choir, glee club, marching band, orchestra, cheerleading team, or popular music group; practicing aerobics, modeling, or sports; participating in a talent or variety show, skit, or play; joining student council or a debate team; serving as an assistant in a theater arts or communications department; running for political office or competing in an oratory contest; reading publications related to the performing arts.

Skills

- Ability to concentrate and practice intensely for long periods of time
- Ability to speak articulately, listen introspectively, and make keen observations
- Good health, physical stamina, and body coordination
- Ability to work well under pressure and meet deadlines
- Ability to maintain composure when faced with the unexpected
- Ability to communicate emotions and ideas creatively
- Ability to relate to people of varying backgrounds
- Proficiency in memorization
- Ability to attract the attention of others
- Ability to analyze and interpret the emotions and motives of others

Values and Attributes

- Aesthetic awareness
- Independence
- Self-expression and fulfillment
- Desire for recognition and influence
- Creativity
- Ability to withstand close scrutiny and criticism from the public
- Ability to adjust to ups and downs
- Sense of drama and showmanship
- Physical stamina
- Patience
- Determination
- Imagination
- Self-discipline
- Analytical mind
- Dedication
- Poise

Resources

- Moore, Dick. *Opportunities in Acting Careers.* VGM Career Horizons, 1999.
- **National Association of Schools of Theater**
  250 Roger Bacon Drive, Suite 21
  Reston, VA 22091
  703-437-6312
  (accrediting agency for postsecondary programs in theater)
- **Screen Actors Guild**
  5757 Wilshire Boulevard
  Los Angeles, CA 90036
  213-954-1600
  http://www.sag.com/
  (publishes *Hollywood Call Sheet* and *Screen Actor,* both of which may be of interest to aspiring actors)
- **Theater Communications Group**
  355 Lexington Avenue
  New York, NY 10017
  212-697-5230
  (promotes nonprofit theaters and theater artists, awards annual grants, operates artist residency programs, and offers *Basic Information for Those Considering a Professional Acting Career*)

Philosophy

Philosophy is considered a branch of the language arts and involves the study of the truths or principles underlying all knowledge. Philosophical study involves the analysis, interpretation, and logical explanation of what humans believe, value, and do. While related occupations are generally only indirectly linked to the study of philosophy, a number of other disciplines, avocations, and leisure activities offer additional pursuits for interested students. Among the major sub-branches are metaphysics (what is real?), logic (what is truth?, what is knowledge?), and axiology (what is good? moral? bad? beautiful?).

High School Courses

Literature	History
Religion	Language Arts
Debate	Forensics
English	Social Studies
Sociology	Anthropology
Psychology	Government
Philosophy	

Related Occupations

Anthropologist—-D	College Administrator—-B/D
College Instructor—-M/D	Diplomat—-B
Film Editor—-AA	Foreign Correspondent—-B
Freelance Writer—-B	Historian—-B/D
Journalist—-B	Judge—-P
Lawyer—-P	Lecturer—-B/M
Librarian—-M	Market Research Analyst—-B
Political Scientist—-B/D	Psychologist—-D
Public Administrator—-B	Publisher—-B
Research Assistant—-B	Social Worker—-B/M

Leisure Activities

Participating on a debate or forensics team; freelance writing; playing word games and games of strategy; participating in oratory contests; joining a philosophical organization such as the American Philosophical Association; subscribing to professional publications related to philosophy; visiting libraries; working part-time or as a volunteer research assistant or in a philosophy department; attending lectures; listening to radio talk shows; participating in political campaigns; joining a student government or student association group.

Skills

- Ability to formulate and defend positions
- Ability to make keen observations, evaluations, and appropriate decisions
- Ability to summarize complicated materials and solve problems
- Ability to concentrate for long periods of time
- Ability to speak articulately
- Objectivity
- Ability to organize, conduct, and clearly explain research
- Proficiency in analytical reasoning
- Ability to synthesize information
- Broad background of general knowledge
- Comprehensive command of grammar and vocabulary

Values and Attributes

- Intellectual growth
- Logical thought and self-expression
- Desire for recognition and to influence others
- Independence
- Tendency to question and seek answers
- Tendency to support beliefs with facts and logic
- Thoughtfulness
- Persuasiveness
- Objectivity
- Imagination

Resources

- Nadler, Burt. *Liberal Arts Jobs: The Guide That Turns Learning into Earning, Third Edition.* Peterson's, 1998.
- **American Philosophical Association**
  University of Delaware
  Newark, DE 19716
  302-831-1112
  http://www.vael.edu/apa/
  (publishes *A Nonacademic Career?, The Philosophy Major,* and *So, You Want to Teach Precollege Philosophy?*)
- **Society of Christian Philosophers**
  Calvin College, Department of Philosophy
  3201 Burton Street, SE
  Grand Rapids, MI 49546
  http://www.siu.edu/departments/cola/philos/scp
  (provides forum for discussion of Christian and philosophical issues)

Physics

Physics is a major branch of the physical sciences and involves the study of matter and energy. It attempts to find out how and why physical matter and energy interact as well as how to describe force, motion, and gravity. Physics is considered to be the foundation of science and technology. It is closely related to astronomy, engineering, chemistry, mathematics, geology, and biology.

High School Courses

Science   Earth Science
Physical Science   Biology
Chemistry   Physics
Math   Algebra
Geometry   Trigonometry
Calculus   Statistics

Related Occupations

Aerodynamist—-B/D   Aeronautical Engineer—-B
Aerospace Engineer—-B/D   Airplane Pilot—-AA/D
Astronomer—-B/D   Astrophysicist—-B/D
Biophysicist—-B   Civil Engineer—-B
Computer Programmer—-B   Educator—-B/D
Electrical Engineer—-B   Environmental Engineer—-B
Geophysicist—-B/D   Laboratory Technician—-AA
Mathematician—-B/D   Metallurgical Engineer—-B
Metallurgist—-B   Meteorologist—-B
Nuclear Engineer—-B/D   Nuclear Medical Technologist—-AA
Nuclear Technician—-AA   Optical Technician—-AA
Physicist—-B/D   Seismologist—-B

Leisure Activities

Joining a photography club, the American Physical Society, the Society of Physics Students, or another physics club; participating in outdoor activities or sports; reading physics or science publications; computer programming; operating a ham radio; repairing radios, TVs, or stereos; playing board games and doing puzzles; performing lab experiments; solving analytic and logic problems.

Skills

- Ability to organize, analyze, and interpret scientific data
- Intellectual capacity to perform well in most undergraduate and graduate college programs
- Ability to make keen observations and appropriate decisions
- Ability to conduct and clearly explain scientific research
- Proficiency with computers
- Aptitude for accuracy and detail
- Proficiency in questioning and problem solving
- Proficiency in reading, writing, memorization, and speaking
- Strong background in mathematics
- Good vision and manual dexterity

Values and Attributes

- Achievement
- Independence
- Intellectual growth
- Recognition
- Strong desire to know why and how things work
- Fondness for mathematics and science
- Analytical mind
- Curiosity
- Dedication
- Imagination
- Perseverance

Resources

- **Amateur Astronomers Association**
  1010 Park Avenue
  New York, NY 10028
  212-535-2922
  (offers educational programs, lectures, and seminars, constellation study, field trips, and more)
- **American Institute of Physics**
  One Physics Ellipse
  College Park, MD 20740
  301-209-3100
  http://www.aip.org/
  (ask about career planning and career information offerings)
- **American Physical Society**
  One Physics Ellipse
  College Park, MD 20740
  301-209-0863
  http://www.aps.org/
  (provides career and employment service and information on minority scholarships and women in physics)

Physiology

Physiology is a branch of the biological sciences that involves the study of life processes and functions. This study requires the close observation, recording, and analysis of cellular and sub-cellular constructions, tissues, and organs to understand how they function and why. Research into the way these systems respond within and between organisms and to environmental influences is important to physiological study. Major branches of this discipline include plant and animal physiology. Physiology also overlaps with chemistry, physics, and mathematics.

High School Courses

Science	Biology
Physiology	Chemistry
Physics	Algebra
Geometry	Trigonometry
Health	First Aid

Related Occupations

Anatomist—-B	Anesthesiologist—-B
Biochemist—-B	Biophysicist—-B/D
Botanist—-B	Cardiologist—-D
Chemist—-B/D	Dietitian—-B
Emergency Medical Technician—-AA	Funeral Director—-AA/B
Geneticist—-B	Gynecologist—-D
Internist—-P	Medical Assistant—-AA
Microbiologist—-B/D	Nutritionist—-B
Osteopath—-P	Pathologist—-D
Pediatrician—-D	Pharmacist—-B
Pharmacologist—-B	Physician Assistant—-AA/B
Physiologist—-B/D	Psychiatrist—-D
Respiratory Therapist—-AA	Surgeon—-P
Toxicologist—-B/D	Urologist—-D
Veterinarian—-D	

Leisure Activities

Attending science fairs or exhibits; visiting museums or zoos; reading science journals, magazines, and books; joining a health club; doing lab experiments and researching science-related topics; volunteering for the American Red Cross, American Cancer Society, or a local mental health association, hospital, or nursing home; owning or caring for pets; watching medical shows on TV or at a theater; actively or financially supporting blood donor drives or medical research efforts.

Skills

- Ability to concentrate for long periods of time
- Ability to conduct and clearly explain scientific research
- Ability to make keen observations and appropriate decisions
- Ability to work under pressure
- Good understanding of mathematical principles and basic knowledge of chemistry and physics
- Proficiency in reading, writing, speaking, and memorizing
- Intellectual capacity to perform well in most undergraduate and graduate college programs
- Thorough knowledge of basic biological theories and practices
- Proficiency in critical thinking, analysis, and problem solving
- Physical stamina, good vision, and manual dexterity

Values and Attributes

- Achievement
- Creativity
- Helpful attitude
- Independence
- Intellectual growth
- Prestige
- Desire to help improve our world
- Interest in public health and safety
- Strong interest in how and why living organisms function
- Curiosity
- Empathy
- Endurance
- Patience
- Persistence
- Self-discipline
- Thoroughness

Resources

- Sacks, Terence. *Careers in Medicine: Second Edition.* VGM Career Horizons, 1997.

- **American Physiological Society**
  9650 Rockville Pike
  Bethesda, MD 20814
  301-530-7164
  http://www.faseb.org/aps/
  (offers student memberships and provides valuable information in its career opportunities department)

- **American Society for Microbiology**
  1325 Massachusetts Avenue, NW
  Washington, DC 20005
  202-942-9346
  http://www.asmusa.org/
  (sponsors a career forum and placement service; provides career development information; offers student membership; publishes *Employment Outlook in the Microbiological Sciences*)

Political Science

Political science is the study of government and focuses on its structure and function and the need for human social order. Political science study attempts to provide students with a better understanding of political parties, interest groups, international relationships, public law, public administration, liberty, freedom, justice, and power. Major sub-branches include political theory and philosophy, comparative government, American government and politics, public administration, international relations, and political behavior.

High School Courses

Civics

Social Studies

Sociology

Public Speaking

Debate

English

Government

Psychology

History

Speech

Forensics

Related Occupations

Announcer—-B

Chamber of Commerce Manager—-B

Diplomat—-B/M

FBI/CIA Agent—-B/M

Geographer—-B/D

Labor Relations Specialist—-B

Lobbyist—-B

Military Officer—-B

Parole/Probation Officer—-B

Political Consultant—-B

Politician—-B

Public Health Official—-B

School Administrator—-B

Technical Writer—-B

Campaign Worker—-V

City Manager—-B

Educator—-B/D

Foreign Service Officer—-B/M

Judge—-P

Lawyer—-P

Mayor—-V

News Reporter—-B

Penologist—-B

Political Scientist—-B/D

Public Recreation Director—-B

Research Assistant—-B

Surveying Technician—-V

Urban Planner—-B

Leisure Activities

Attending political rallies or lectures; serving as a part-time worker or volunteer precinct clerk, party worker, or poll watcher; running for or serving in a public school or municipal office; joining a debate or forensics team; participating in fund-raising or writing promotional materials for a political campaign; joining a student government; chairing a public panel discussion; working part-time or as a volunteer news broadcaster for a school radio or TV station; joining a school newspaper staff; participating in a neighborhood association; freelance writing; reading political publications; joining a professional group such as the American Political Science Association.

Skills

- Ability to conduct and clearly explain scientific research clearly
- Ability to effectively communicate ideas to others
- Intellectual capacity to perform well in most undergraduate and graduate programs
- Ability to relate to people from varying backgrounds
- Ability to speak articulately, read comprehensively, and write well
- Charisma and public appeal
- Aptitude for leadership
- Ability to organize and interpret social, economic, and political data
- Understanding of and sensitivity to community needs
- Broad background of general knowledge
- Ability to effectively evaluate problems and make appropriate decisions

Values and Attributes

- Achievement
- Desire for recognition and to influence others
- Prestige
- Tendency to be ambitious and outgoing
- Desire to render public service
- Willingness to take risks
- Poise
- Tactfulness
- Patience
- Perseverance
- Flexibility
- Competitive drive

Resources

- Camenson, Blythe. *Real People Working in Government.* VGM Career Horizons, 1998.
- **American Political Science Association**
  1527 New Hampshire Avenue, NW
  Washington, DC 20036
  202-483-2512
  http://www.apsanet.org/
  (offers job placement service and publishes *American Political Science Review*)
- **National Association of Schools of Public Affairs and Administration**
  1120 G Street NW, Suite 730
  Washington, DC 20005
  202-628-8965
  http://www.naspaa.org/
  (offers information about accreditation, schools, and public service)

Psychology

Psychology is the study of human and animal behavior. It seeks to understand and explain both normal and abnormal behavior, mental ability, perception, development, and differences in individuals. Psychological study also explores human emotions, thoughts, and motives. Among the major sub-branches within this field are educational psychology, social psychology, psychometrics, developmental psychology, comparative psychology, psychology of the personality, abnormal psychology, applied psychology, differential psychology, statistics, and child psychology.

High School Courses

Social Studies	Sociology
Psychology	History
Economics	Government
Religion	Health

Related Occupations

Advertising Manager—-B	Educator—-B/D
Employee Assistance Administrator—-B	
Employment Counselor—-B	Guidance Counselor—-M
Human Resource Manager—-B	Industrial Psychologist—-M/D
Job Analyst—-B	Market Research Analyst—-B
Mental Health Worker—-B	Minister—-P/V
Occupational Therapist—-B	Outplacement Specialist—-B/D
Penologist—-B	Police Officer—-AA
Probation Officer—-B	Psychiatric Nurse—-B
Psychiatric Social Worker—-M	Psychiatrist—-P
Psychologist—-D	Psychometrist—-B/M
Public Relations Specialist—-B	Speech Pathologist—-M
Vocational Rehabilitation Counselor—-B/M	

Leisure Activities

Serving as a peer advisor; working part-time or as a volunteer in a mental health agency, psychology department, or senior citizens' home; assisting with college recruitment efforts; serving on a student council or as a tutor; participating in Junior Achievement; serving as a leader or chairperson in a community or school organization; working part-time or as a volunteer in an advertising firm, sales department, special education class, or day care center; serving as a camp counselor or hotline assistant; freelance writing; reading psychology-related publications.

Skills

- Ability to interpret and clearly explain psychological research and tests of all types
- Proficiency in reading comprehension, writing, and speaking
- Understanding of human development and behavior
- Ability to observe and analyze introspectively
- Sensitivity to and understanding of the needs and emotions of others
- Ability to evaluate personal problems and make appropriate decisions
- Intellectual capacity to do well in most undergraduate or graduate college programs
- Proficiency in interpersonal communication

Values and Attributes

- Intellectual understanding
- Helpfulness
- Mental and emotional well-being
- Sensitivity to the inconsistencies of human behavior
- Desire to continue learning throughout life
- Warm and personable character
- Tactfulness
- Inquisitiveness
- Integrity
- Patience

Resources

- Sternberg, Robert. *Career Paths in Psychology.* American Psychology, 1997.
- **American Psychological Association**
  750 First Street, NE
  Washington, DC 20002
  202-336-5500
  http://www.apa.org/
  (provides information about psychology careers—including nonacademic careers—minority interests, useful skills, salaries, and scholarships)
- **National Association of School Psychologists**
  4340 East-West Highway, Suite 402
  Bethesda, MD 20814
  301-657-0270
  http://www.naspweb.org/
  (offers scholarships and publishes *What Is a School Psychologist?*)

Recreation and Leisure

Recreation and leisure focuses on the design, management, implementation, supervision, expansion of, and need for recreational and leisure activities among individuals and groups of all ages and backgrounds. The recreation and leisure field encompasses a broad range of events and activities related to camping, natural resources, outdoor activities, tourism, amusement parks, sporting events, and community recreation programs. A few of the many specialties within this growing field are gerontology, youth organizations, parks and forestry, public recreation, tourism, commercial enterprising, therapeutic recreation, professional sports, resource management, recreation, and parks administration.

High School Courses

Physical Education

First Aid

Arts

Sociology

Health

Theater

Social Studies

Psychology

Related Occupations

Armed Forces Recreation Leader—-AA

Athletic Trainer—-B

Church Recreation Director—-V

Coach—-V

Community Center Director—-AA/B

Dance Instructor—-B/V

Exercise Physiologist—-B

Game Official—-B

Municipal Recreation Director—-B

Park Ranger—-B

Playground Leader—-AA

Professional Athlete—-V

Recreation Therapist—-B

Ski Instructor—-V

Sports Reporter—-B

Camp Director—-B

Circus Performer—-V

College Recreation Instructor—-B/M

Concert Promoter—-B/V

Dance Therapist—-B

Fitness Instructor/Specialist—-B

Lifeguard—-V/AA

Music Therapist—-B

Physical Education Instructor—-B

Prison Recreation Specialist—-B

Recreation Facility Manager—-B

Resort Manager—-B

Sports Marketer—-B

Leisure Activities

Playing or participating in sports; working as a camp counselor or at a fitness club, playground, or other recreational facility; engaging in physical and outdoor activities; serving as a part-time coach, official, or scorer; reading publications related to recreation, sports, health, and fitness; organizing and participating in community recreational activities; attending lectures and workshops related to recreation and leisure; serving as an aide in a school physical education or recreation department.

Skills

- Ability to relate to and interact with people of varying ages and backgrounds
- Ability to lead, supervise, and direct others
- Ability to react spontaneously and maintain emotional composure in stressful situations
- Understanding of human nature
- Good health, vision, and physical stamina
- Ability to solve problems and make appropriate decisions
- Proficiency in written and oral communication
- Ability to organize and coordinate activities
- General knowledge of recreational and leisure theories and practices
- A high level of athletic ability (for a career as a fitness instructor or athlete)

Values and Attributes

- Health
- Achievement
- Emotional well-being
- Sensitivity to the human need for recreation and balance
- A good sense of humor and fondness for being around people
- Friendliness
- Tactfulness
- Dedication
- Patience
- Outgoing personality

Resources

- Camenson, Blythe. *Opportunities in Summer Camp Careers.* VGM Career Horizons, 1998.
- *What Can I Do Now? Preparing for a Career in Sports.* Ferguson Publishing Company, 1998.
- **American Alliance for Health, Physical Education, Recreation, and Dance**
  1900 Association Drive
  Reston, VA 22091
  703-476-3400
  http://www.aahperd.org/
  (offers scholarships, student membership, and career information and publishes a student newsletter)
- **National Recreation and Park Association**
  22377 Belmont Ridge Road
  Ashburn, VA 20148
  703-858-0784
  http://www.nrpa.org/
  (has a professional career center that provides information about university programs, community recreation, natural resources, park management, recreation administration, therapeutic recreation, and more)

Religion and Theology

Religion and theology is the study of human beliefs, practices, and worship activities related to a supreme power or deity. Students are familiarized with religious history, doctrine, theological concepts, and worship practices as well as issues related to faith, love, patience, long-suffering, and forgiveness. Focus may be on a particular denomination or faith or in a specialization such as youth work, religious education, mission work, clerical studies, administration and leadership, evangelism, or outreach.

High School Courses

Bible History

Social Studies

History

Government

Religion

Sociology

Philosophy

Anthropology

Related Occupations

Campus Minister—-B

Chaplain—-D

Director of Religious Education—-B

Minister of Music—-B

Pastor—-P/V

Rabbi—-P

Religious Educational Administrator—-B/V

Religious Education Teacher—-B

Religious Sister—-V/B

Salvation Army Officer—-V/B

Youth Minister—-V/P

Campus Religious Coordinator—-D

Church Camp Director—-B

Evangelist—-V/P

Missionary—-B/V

Priest—-P

Religious Brother—-V/B

Religious Researcher—-B

Religious Writer—-V/B

Social Worker—-B/M

Leisure Activities

Regularly participating in local church activities; working part-time or as a volunteer in a religious institution or bookstore; attending religious retreats, conferences, revivals, or workshops; listening to religious lectures, tapes and music; participating in and financially contributing to religious and charitable endeavors; visiting shut-ins or those who are sick or in jail; belonging to a religious club or fellowship group; attending Bible study; reading publications related to religion or theology; viewing religious programs on TV; engaging in activities that help others.

Skills

- Knowledge and proficiency in some area of personal ministry
- Ability to interact with people of varying ages and backgrounds
- General knowledge of the practices, procedures, guidelines, and doctrine of your faith
- Ability to persuade and influence others
- Ability to carry out and integrate one's occupational responsibilities with your religious faith
- Proficiency in reading, writing, and oral communication
- Proficiency in interpersonal communication
- Understanding of human spiritual and social needs
- Sensitivity to and compassion for others
- Ability to make appropriate decisions and solve problems

Values and Attributes

- Religious faith
- Desire to do God's will and love others
- Wisdom
- Morality
- Willingness to continue learning throughout life
- An inner spiritual conviction or calling to serve in a religious capacity
- Sensitivity and concern for the spiritual welfare of others
- Dedication
- Perseverance
- Integrity
- Faith
- Determination

Resources

- Nelson, John, Ph.D. *Opportunities in Religious Service Careers.* VGM Career Horizons, 1998.
- **Intercristo**
  19303 Fremont Avenue, North
  Seattle, WA 98133
  800-251-7740
  http://www.jobleads.org/
  (offers a Christian job referral service, career ideas, and salary comparisons, and publishes a comprehensive career kit entitled *A Christian's Guide to Career Building*)
- **National Council of Churches**
  475 Riverside Drive, Room 850
  New York, NY 10115
  212-870-2227
  http://ncccusa.org/index.htm/
  (represents 52,000,000 members of Protestant, Anglican, and Orthodox denominations; publishes a variety of religious and educational materials)
- **National Religious Vocation Conference**
  5420 South Cornell Avenue, Suite 105
  Chicago, IL 60615
  773-363-5454
  http://www.visionguide.org
  (offers various materials on religious vocations within the Catholic Church, including the annual *Vision Guide* in print and online)

Secretarial Science

Secretarial science is the study of the administrative, clerical, information management, and human relations skills associated with and necessary for the efficient operation of an office or workplace. Students learn secretarial responsibilities such as typing, filing, stenography, and word processing and other computer programs. Secretarial science students are also introduced to methods of information management, organization, schedule coordination, problem solving, decision-making, accounting, and communication as well as general office procedures. Specialties in this area are legal, medical, executive, technical, and school.

High School Courses

Business	Math
Word Processing	Office Operations/Practices
Business Machines	Bookkeeping
Accounting	English
Speech	Psychology

Related Occupations

Accounting Clerk—-V	Administrative Assistant—-AA
Bank Teller—-V	Cashier—-V
Court Reporter—-AA/B	Data Input Operator—-V
Dental Assistant—-AA	Educational Secretary—-C/AA
Educator—-V/B	Executive Secretary—-AA/B
File Clerk—-V	Foreign Service Secretary—-AA
Legal Secretary—-AA	Medical Assistant—-C/AA
Medical Assistant Secretary—-C/AA	Office Clerk—-AA/B
Office Manager—-AA/B	Paralegal—-AA
Receptionist—-V	Records Manager—-AA
Secretary—-V	Stenographer—-AA
Typist—-AA	Word Processor—-V

Leisure Activities

Working as a part-time or volunteer student aide, secretarial assistant, or office clerk; reading materials on administrative and secretarial careers; volunteering as an office helper for a local church, neighborhood association, club, or community agency; belonging to a student or professional office personnel organization; writing reports and making oral presentations; working on a school newspaper; providing a word processing, telecommuting, resume-writing, or editing service; organizing social events.

Skills

- Good vision and health
- Proficiency for memorization, accuracy, and detail
- Ability to work independently as well as interact effectively with people of different backgrounds
- Ability to work quickly, with distractions, and under tight deadlines
- Ability to take the initiative, make sound judgments and appropriate decisions, and solve problems
- Proficiency with computers
- Strong office skills, including proficiency in operating electronic office equipment like scanners, fax machines, and copiers
- Knowledge of practices and trends in office procedures
- Ability to understand and interpret written and oral communication
- Proficiency in spelling, grammar, punctuation, and editing
- Ability to maintain emotional composure under stressful circumstances

Values and Attributes

- Security
- Recognition
- Achievement
- Neatness and flexibility
- Pleasant, positive, and friendly attitude
- Fairness
- Sense of professionalism
- Willingness to perform tasks that may be repetitive or tedious
- Organization
- Self-confidence
- Dependability
- Tactfulness
- Poise

Resources

- Ettinger, Blanche, Ph.D. *Opportunities in Secretarial Careers.* VGM Career Horizons, 1999.
- **International Assistants and Administrative Professionals**
  10502 NW Ambassador Drive
  Kansas City, MO 64195
  816-891-6600
  http://www.psi.org/default.htm
  (runs job placement service for administrative support personnel and publishes free career booklets on salaries in the field, temporary service, professional trends, and tips for success)

Social Work

Social work is the study of the processes that assist those in our society who are unable to cope with serious personal and social problems. Study in this field is aimed at helping the needy and disadvantaged in such areas as child and drug abuse, juvenile delinquency and crime, hunger, financial budgeting, unemployment, health care, mental illness, disability education, parenting, family problems, and homelessness. Some of the areas of specialization are health care and mental health, education, family services, child welfare, drug abuse, gerontology, clinical, and occupational.

High School Courses

Civics	Government
Social Studies	Sociology
Health	Economics
History	Psychology

Related Occupations

Child Welfare Worker—-B	Community Service Agency Director—-B
Cooperative Extension Worker—-B	Drug Rehabilitation Counselor—-B
Educator—-M/D	Employee-Assistance Administrator—-M
Family Services Social Worker—-B	Geriatric Case Worker—-M
Gerontologist—-B/D	Group Home Director—-AA/B
Home Economist—-B	Human Services Worker—-B
Marriage Counselor—-B	Minister—-P
Peace Corps/VISTA Volunteer—-B	Probation Officer—-B
Psychiatric Social Worker—-M	Psychologist—-D ·
Residential Counselor—-AA	School Counselor—-M
School Psychologist—-D	Social Service Aide—-AA
Social Service Director—-M	Social Worker—-B/M
Sociologist—-D	Technical Writer—-B
Vocational Rehabilitation Counselor—-M	

Leisure Activities

Working part-time or as a volunteer in a community social agency; participating in charitable outreach endeavors and church activities; serving as a peer counselor, tutor, or hotline assistant; donating money toward social concerns; reading publications that focus on social problems and issues; belonging to a professional organization such as the National Association of Social Workers, Inc.; attending lectures and conferences related to social work; participating in a Big Brother/Big Sister program.

Skills

- Understanding of human behavior and familiarity with community services
- Familiarity with social work theories, practices and trends
- Ability to interact with people of different backgrounds in a variety of situations
- Proficiency in interpersonal communication
- Intellectual capacity to do well in most undergraduate and graduate college programs
- Proficiency in reading comprehension, writing, and speaking
- Ability to respond spontaneously and maintain composure in stressful situations
- Ability to keenly observe, evaluate, and solve problems
- Ability to conduct and clearly explain social research
- Ability to make appropriate decisions and sound judgments

Values and Attributes

- Achievement
- Desire for recognition and appreciation from others
- Desire to work directly with those challenged by social problems
- Sensitivity to the needs and pains of others
- Ability to work under unpleasant and stressful conditions
- Patience
- Resourcefulness
- Empathy
- Tactfulness
- Integrity
- Discretion

Resources

- Krannich, Ron and Caryl, Ph.D.'s. *Jobs & Careers with Nonprofit Organizations: Profitable Opportunities with Nonprofits, Second Edition.* Impact Publications, 1999.
- Wittenberg, Renee. *Opportunities in Social Work.* VGM Career Horizons, 1997.
- **American Association of State Social Work Boards**
  400 S. Ridge Parkway, Suite B
  Culpeper, VA 22701
  540-829-6880
  http://www.aasswb.org/
  (provides information about licensure and certification standards as well as examination study guides and registration materials)
- **National Association of Social Workers**
  750 First Street, NE, Suite 700
  Washington, DC 20002
  202-408-8600
  http://www.naswdc.org/
  (provides information about accredited schools, licensure, and social work careers)

Sociology

Sociology is the study of social life and focuses on the interaction between human groups and institutions and their influences on each other. Sociology ranges from the study of relationships in family units in the most primitive cultures to the research of large bureaucratic institutions in major industrialized nations. Among the specialties within sociology are criminology, demography, cultural traditions, family relations, social psychology, gerontology, social welfare, race relations, education, social status, and social change.

High School Courses

Civics

Social Studies

Health

History

Anthropology

Government

Sociology

Religion

Economics

Psychology

Related Occupations

Anthropologist—-M/D

City Manager—-B

Counselor—-M

Demographer—-B

Foreign Service Worker—-V ✓

Historian—-M/D

Labor Relations Specialist—-B

Peace Corps/VISTA Volunteer—-B ✓

Probation Officer—-B

Public Administrator—-B

Research Assistant—-B

Sociologist—-D

Urban Planner—-B

Case Worker—-AA

Consultant—-D

Criminologist—-B

Educator—-B/D

Gerontologist—-B

Human Services Worker—-V/B

Minister—-P/V

Political Scientist—-B/D

Psychologist—-D

Public Relations Manager—-B

Social Worker—-B/M

Surveying Technician—-AA/B

Leisure Activities

Participating in charitable outreach endeavors; joining church activities; donating money toward social concerns; working as a part-time or volunteer peer counselor in a day care center or community service agency; organizing games, parties, or get-togethers; joining a professional organization such as the American Sociological Association; serving as a camp counselor, on a school board, or as a social research aide; freelance writing; reading social-issues publications; joining a school or community club.

Skills

- Proficiency in interpersonal communication
- Intellectual capacity to do well in most undergraduate and graduate college programs
- Ability to conduct and clearly explain sociological research
- Ability to interact with people of different backgrounds in various situations
- Knowledge of community resources
- Ability to maintain composure in stressful situations
- Proficiency in reading comprehension, writing, and speaking
- Ability to evaluate problems and make appropriate decisions
- Proficiency with computers

Values and Attributes

- Desire for recognition and appreciation from others
- Desire to help humanity
- Intellectual growth
- Strong interest in human problems and events
- Sensitivity to and understanding of social problems
- Desire to solve social problems
- Curiosity
- Resourcefulness
- Empathy
- Tactfulness
- Integrity
- Independence

Resources

- Marek, Rosanne. *Opportunities in Social Science Careers*. VGM Career Horizons, 1997.
- **American Sociological Association**

  1722 N Street, NW

  Washington, DC 20036

  202-785-0146

  http://www.asanet.org/

  (offers student membership and develops materials for those interested in teaching and research and in applied sociology)
- **Sociological Practice Association**

  Anne Arundel Community College

  Division of Social Science

  101 College Parkway

  Arnold, MD 21012

  410-541-2835

  (publishes newsletter called "Practicing Sociologist")

Transportation

Transportation is the field that focuses on the movement of people, materials, and equipment from one place to another. The logistics required for the numerous methods of transportation in an industrialized society are complex. Study in transportation concentrates on how automobiles, buses, trucks, trains, waterways, airplanes, pipelines, and industrial equipment are scientifically, technologically, and creatively manipulated to effectively meet the location needs and deadlines of materials and people. Transportation students specialize in such areas as trucking, automobiles, busing, railroads, waterways, construction machine operating, industrial machine operation, and aircraft.

High School Courses

Business
Physical Education
Health Mathematics
Statistics

Economics
Driver's Education

Related Occupations

Airplane Pilot—-AA/B
Ambulance Driver—-V
Chauffeur—-V
Deep Submergence Vehicle Operator—-AA
Dispatcher—-AA
Educator—-B/D
Industrial Truck Operator—-V
Merchant Mariner—-AA/B
Oil Pumper—-V
Physical Distribution Manager—-B
Taxi Driver—-V
Train Conductor—-V
Truck Driver—-V

Air Traffic Controller—-AA
Bus Driver—-V
Coal Pipe Line Operator—-V

Driving Instructor—-V
Ferryboat Operator—-V
Locomotive Engineer—-V
Motorboat Operator—-V
Operating Engineer—-V
Service Station Worker—-V
Traffic Manager—-B
Transportation Engineer—-B

Leisure Activities

Working part-time in a service station, parking garage, or at a truck, bus, or airport terminal; engaging in activities that involve moving, hauling, or driving; reading publications related to transportation; developing hobbies, collections, and interests related to model cars, trains, or other vehicles; participating in or visiting racing events, or car, truck, or boat shows or exhibits; operating farm equipment.

Skills

- Ability to clearly understand and apply instructions for operating vehicular or mobile equipment
- Manual dexterity and mechanical aptitude
- Aptitude for accuracy and detail
- Knowledge of transportation and safety codes and regulations in an area of specialization
- Good health and physical stamina
- Good vision, color perception, and eye-hand-foot coordination
- Ability to give and understand directions
- Ability to make keen observations, sound judgments, and appropriate decisions
- Ability to react quickly, work under pressure, and meet deadlines

Values and Attributes

- Power
- Sense of adventure
- Achievement
- Ability to work in stressful situations and awkward positions
- Enjoyment and appreciation of the importance of moving and maintaining vehicles and equipment
- Enjoyment of challenges
- Patience
- Responsibility
- Dependability
- Competence
- Endurance
- Alertness

Resources

- Paradis, Adrian. *Opportunities in Transportation Careers.* VGM Career Horizons, 1997.
- Heitzmann, William. *Opportunities in Marine and Maritime Careers.* VGM Career Horizons, 1999.
- **Air Transport Association of America**
  30 Pennsylvania Avenue, NW, Suite 0
  Washington, DC 20004
  202-626-4000
  http://www.air.transport.org/
  (organization of airlines that transport persons and goods)
- **American Public Transit Association**
  1201 New York Avenue, NW, Suite 400
  Washington, DC 20005
  202-898-4000
  http://www.apta.com/
  (offers scholarships and publishes newsletter that lists job opportunities)
- **American Trucking Association**
  2200 Mill Road
  Alexandria, VA 22314
  703-838-873
  http://truckline.com/
  (the customer services area offers a free brochure entitled *Careers in Truck Driving*)
- **Brotherhood of Locomotive Engineers**
  1370 Ontario Avenue, Mezzanine
  Cleveland, OH 44113
  216-241-2630
  (sponsors educational seminars)

Zoology

Zoology is a major branch of the biological sciences and involves the study of animals. Zoology ranges from the subatomic and cellular level of the smallest organism to the largest mammal. Zoological study focuses on embryonic development, body structure and function of parts, habitat, and ecological interactions with other living organisms. Specializations within this subject include embryology, cytology, ecology, entomology, ornithology, anatomy, physiology, paleontology, genetics, herpetology, parasitology, mammalogy, marine biology, and wildlife fisheries biology.

High School Courses

Science

Physiology

Math

Geometry

Biology

Chemistry

Algebra

Related Occupations

Animal Breeder—-V

Animal Laboratory Technician—-AA

Conservationist—-B

Ecologist—-B

Farm/Ranch Manager—-B/V

Forester—-B

Kennel Operator—-V

Microbiologist—-B

Nature Photographer—-AA/B

Pathologist—-D

Pet Shop Manager—-V

Range Manager—-AA/B

Technical Writer—-B

Veterinary Assistant—-V/AA

Zookeeper—-AA/B

Animal Control Officer—-AA

Biochemist—-B

Curator—-B

Educator—-B/D

Fishery Biologist—-B

Humane Society Worker—-AA

Marine Biologist—-B

Museum/Zoo Worker—-AA

Park Ranger—-B

Pest Control Worker—-AA

Public Health Specialist—-B

Taxonomist—-B

Veterinarian—-P

Wildlife Biologist—-B

Zoologist—-B/D

Leisure Activities

Browsing through 4-H exhibits, pet shops, and science displays; attending animal shows or the circus; belonging to a zoological society, Future Farmers of America or wildlife preservation group, or the Humane Society; visiting aquariums, museums, zoos, and nature centers; hiking, camping, nature photography, bird-watching, fishing, or horseback riding; owning and caring for pets; working part-time or as a volunteer for the American Society for the Prevention of Cruelty to Animals, the Humane Society, or a national park or forest, zoo, or veterinary office; watching animal shows on TV; reading animal-related publications; collecting shells, butterflies, insects, or other natural specimens.

Skills

- Proficiency in observing, collecting, and analyzing data
- Ability to concentrate for long periods of time
- Proficiency in reading, writing, speaking, and memorization
- Ability to conduct and clearly explain scientific research
- Proficiency in problem solving and decision-making
- Proficiency for accuracy and detail
- Ability to work with and relate to animals
- Intellectual capacity to perform well in most undergraduate and graduate college programs
- Thorough knowledge of general biology
- Good health, physical stamina, agility, and manual dexterity

Values and Attributes

- Achievement
- Desire to help others
- Creativity
- Courage, respect and determination
- Deep appreciation for and kindness toward animals
- Interest in animal protection and preservation
- Curiosity
- Endurance
- Patience
- Perseverance
- Self-control
- Compassion

Resources

- Camenson, Blythe. *Opportunities in Zoo Careers*. VGM Career Horizons, 1998.
- Rejnis, Ruth. *Careers with Creatures Great and Small*. Howell Books, 1999.
- **American Association of Zoo Veterinarians**
  6 North Pennell Road
  Media, PA 19063
  610-892-4812
  http://www.worldzoo.org/aazv/
  (offers student membership)
- **American Zoo and Aquariums Association**
  8403 Coleville Road, Suite 710
  Silver Springs, MD 20910
  301-562-0777
  http://www.aza.org
  (lists employment opportunities and publishes information about careers in zoos and aquariums as well as in mammal, aquatic, and marine science)
- **Society for Integrative and Comparative Biology**
  401 North Michigan Avenue
  Chicago, IL 60611
  312-527-6697
  http://www.sicb.org/
  (maintains a career opportunity desk at annual meetings, offers student membership and educational programs, and publishes *Careers in Animal Biology*)

Section V

Career-Related Questions and Answers

1   What does the word *career* mean?

For many, career means the part of life that is concerned with employment. From an occupational standpoint, it means the sum total of the various jobs one may hold during his or her lifetime. However, these definitions do not fully capture the meaning of career. We would like you to think of career in a broader, more life-encompassing way. Think of the decisions you make about a job or a college major as valuable components of a lifelong process. When viewed in this manner, career can be defined as the sum total of decisions that direct your educational, social, economic, political, and religious endeavors and reflect your unique personality characteristics and basic life values.

2   What is career decision-making?

You can best understand good decision-making by first defining the term decision. A decision can be defined as the act of choosing. A decision, whether you are aware of it or not, is a response to a question, concern, or problem. Appropriate career decisions can be further defined as the ongoing lifelong process of making choices that complement your personal attributes and help you to realize your basic life values. Indeed, career decisions (particularly those pertaining to an occupation) should be made with great care, for they will significantly influence your direction, personal satisfaction, and fulfillment in life.

3   Is career development different for an older adult than for a younger person?

While the basics of career development (self-assessment, decision-making, occupational awareness, exploration, and implementation) are the same regardless of age, variations in maturity and life experiences necessitate different approaches. Some career specialists believe that most adults, like children and young people, go through a number of developmental stages. Consequently, they consider the life stage of a person before selecting a counseling intervention strategy.

4 What is career success?

It really depends on the individual. For some, career success is measured by financial and material accumulation. Others base career success on recognition and popularity. Still others believe that real career success comes only through helping others or doing God's will.

It is my belief that career success comes when you achieve inner satisfaction (reflected in a generally positive attitude) through the continuing realization....

■ of your deepest and most cherished life values in every major endeavor (home, work, school, and leisure).

■ that you have the opportunity and inspiration to use and develop current and desired skills.

■ that you are excited about what you have achieved, are achieving, and can achieve in the future.

5 What is a career resource or information center?

A career resource or information center is an office or agency that provides users with career and life development information, materials, and services. Career resource or information centers can be either public or private; they can be independent or part of a larger institution. Many such centers are located on college campuses and within placement services. Others are found in libraries and high schools. The goal of most centers is to maintain accurate, up-to-date career information and provide support services like seminars and workshops, which enable the user to make more effective life and career decisions.

6 Are career development and placement services the same?

Not really. However, career development and placement services are often cited by many in the same breath. This is understandable in light of their close relationship. Services and programs often overlap and many colleges and universities offer career development and placement functions jointly through the same office. Nevertheless, while there are a number of program similarities, there are several distinguishing characteristics. Career development is primarily concerned with helping the individual to make the most appropriate decisions to assure a fulfilling life. Job placement, on the other hand, focuses on helping a person to actually locate a position and participate and succeed in both career- and noncareer-related work. One might refer to career development as the beginning or foundation stage of the career development and placement process while referring to job placement as the final or practical application stage. However, particularly in America, both functions are usually intertwined in realizing a more meaningful life.

7 What are career development services?

Career development services usually offer the following:

- Life and career advising, consultation, and counseling
- Computerized career guidance activities
- Administration and interpretation of career interest and personality surveys and ability and achievement tests.
- Access to up-to-date occupational files and a career resource library
- Seminars and workshops related to self-awareness, decision-making, goal-setting, and other career development areas
- Development and distribution of career-related handouts and similar materials
- Access to test information files
- Career lectures presented to classrooms and community groups.
- Career information to school administration, faculty, students, and the community at large
- Help in appropriately integrating homelife, work, and leisure activities

8 What are job placement services?

Job placement services usually offer the following:

- Employment advice and counseling
- Information about local, state, and national job openings
- Placement of individuals into part-time and full-time jobs
- Creation and maintenance of individual qualification files
- Job hunting, resume, and interviewing services (including via computer)
- On-campus interviews with potential employers
- Creation and maintenance of employer information files
- Information about career fairs and career days
- Help in establishing professional relationships with local employers
- Information about internships, co-ops, work-study experiences, and on-site visitations
- Follow-up studies related to job placement results and trends
- Lectures to groups on and off campus on job hunting, labor market trends, and other pertinent topics

9 What does a good career counselor do?

Most of the information cited below was developed by the National Career Development Association (NCDA), which can be contacted at http://ncda.org/

- Conducts individual and group counseling sessions to help clarify life and career goals
- Administers and interprets tests and inventories to assess abilities and interests and to identify career options
- Encourages exploratory activities through assignments and planning exercises
- Evaluates, organizes, and provides educational, occupational, and personal resources and information to clients engaged in life development

- Utilizes career planning and occupational information systems to help individuals better understand the world of work
- Helps to improve decision-making skills
- Assists in developing individualized career plans
- Assists with job-search planning and resume development
- Fosters an understanding of the integration of work and other life roles
- Provides support for persons experiencing job stress, job loss, or career transition

10 What is a self-assessment?

A self-assessment entails a serious and honest look at yourself. Self-assessment is a process that requires prioritizing, deep thinking, discovery, and acceptance of personal realities. It may or may not include the help of a career counselor. However, if you want to conduct your assessment in a comprehensive manner, it is strongly recommended that you secure the assistance of a qualified professional. It is not always easy to identify personal aspects of oneself or to use the information discovered to make effective life-changing decisions. However, once you successfully start this process (and it is an ongoing process), it can result in a more focused and fulfilling life. At minimum, self-assessment should include the accurate identification of physical and personal attributes, temperament, abilities and aptitudes, strengths and weaknesses, attitudes, life values, work values, interests, and goals.

Once you have identified, defined, and summarized the above in writing, you will have a beginning "blueprint" of who you are and what you want in life. You can then compare your decisions with this self-assessment to determine how close they are. Keep in mind that you will need to continually monitor, revise, and update your "blueprint." This will ensure that it stays current with your changing reality.

11 What is a college major?

A college major is a specialized field of study which usually reflects one's strongest interests and involves the largest number of courses. While the term major applies to college or university study, its equivalent would be the largest concentration of related courses elected by a student engaged in any postsecondary educational experience (e.g., trade or vocational school, military, etc.).

12 What should I know before selecting a major?

Choosing the appropriate major requires more preparation than many people realize. Contrary to what many think, most of the work needed to effectively select a major should be done prior to entry into a college or university. Ideally, the selection of a major should take place only after you have a fairly good grasp of the techniques for determining, monitoring, and adjusting to who you are and what is most important in your life. Your major area of study should represent only one of a number of important areas in your life, completing the broader life direction previously established. Unfortunately, this advance work is not done by most, resulting in avoidable frustration due to frequent changes in majors as well as wasted time, energy, and money. You can significantly improve your chances of selecting the most appropriate major if you carefully do the following, in order, beforehand:

I. Identify who you are and what is most important to you in life. In other words, conduct a thorough self-assessment, and if necessary, seek the help of a qualified career counselor.

II. Learn the steps of good career decision-making. A good decision-making model might be:

> Step 1: Become aware of the need to make a decision.
> Step 2: Identify what you value, and determine whether or not more information is required.
> Step 3: Gather any additional information you believe is needed to make a more informed and wise decision.
> Step 4: After you have gathered this information, consider the possible results of each alternative.
> Step 5: Select the one alternative that you believe will most appropriately complement the results of your self-assessment.
> Step 6: Develop and implement a plan of action.
> Step 7: If circumstances make it necessary, review and repeat steps 1 through 6.

III. Identify significant factors (including disability, need for more training, family problems, or recent job loss) that you must consider before deciding what you are going to do.

IV. Applying the steps of good decision-making, choose from the following alternatives: enter college or trade school; get married; enter an apprenticeship program; join the military; travel; work for VISTA or the Peace Corps; get a job; keep doing what you are doing. It is only at this point (assuming the results of your self-assessment clearly indicate the need for some type of additional training or education) that you are ready to address the next question...

13 How do I actually select a major?

Choosing a major area of study is often one of the most important (and difficult) decisions a person has to make during his or her lifetime. A genuine effort to determine a suitable major can serve as the catalyst for comprehensive career planning activities. The results can have lifelong implications in terms of learning how to establish and monitor life direction. There are four main steps in the decision-making process. (If you plan to enter a one- or two-year program of study, apprenticeship, or similar endeavor that requires that the major area of study be decided immediately, then you should complete steps 1, 2, and 3 before entry.):

Step 1 requires that you apply the steps of good decision-making to determine what type of curriculum most adequately complements your self-assessment. More than likely—particularly if you have elected to enter a four-year college program—after selecting a suitable curriculum you will find that a number of related majors can possibly "fit." A specific major preference may not crystallize until later.

Usually, this comes about after you have taken a variety of courses, have had fulfilling experiences in certain courses, and have explored several options in-depth through discussions with advisors and reading relevant materials.

Step 2. As you continue to apply the steps of good decision-making, select the training institution, college, or university you believe offers the curriculum and environment that best support your self-assessment and accommodate any significant influencing factors.

Step 3. Next, continuing to apply the steps of good decision-making, select the major that best supports your self-assessment and accommodates any significant influencing factors.

Step 4. Finally, continue to monitor the results of your self-assessment. This is important due to the possibility that one or more significant influencing factors could alter your profile. You should always be ready and willing to refigure previous decisions.

14 What should I do if I want a college degree but don't know what to pick for my major?

Regardless of whether you are in high school or college, there are basic courses that are required in order to earn a diploma or degree. Take these first, as they are likely to apply to the curriculum or major you eventually select (be sure to check the basic requirements in the school's handbook or catalog). In addition to the basics, you may want to take one or more liberal arts or practical electives (computer science, interpersonal communications, writing, speech) that are increasingly important in our changing society. Though these courses may not directly apply to your eventual major or profession, the information acquired can be applied to other areas of your life. Since these courses will be taken at least initially as electives, it is recommended that you don't enroll in too many before you've reached a decision on your curriculum focus. The extra time you gain as a result will provide you with the opportunity to engage in unrushed self-assessment and other career planning activities. Then, the next time you select courses, you can make informed and wise decisions.

15 What should I do if I only want to pursue a short-term program of a year or less?

Most short-term programs are highly specialized, and courses taken rarely transfer to other programs. Entering into a short-term program without a clear indication that it will most realistically support your self-assessment could prove to be a significant waste of time, energy, and money. Therefore, comprehensive career planning activities are recommended before enrolling into any one- or two-year programs. (You can elect to do this yourself or seek help from a qualified career counselor.)

16 I must register for a full load of classes tomorrow but don't know what to take—what should I do?

There are many variables to consider. Do you plan to graduate from this institution? If so, have you completed all of the basic required courses? Do you have self-assessment results from recent career development activities? If so, what courses seem to complement what you know about yourself? Do you have room for electives? Do you want to attend days? Nights? Part-time? Full-time? Try to answer these questions first, then, though it may be difficult to get in to talk with someone, present this concern to a qualified career counselor or academic advisor. Some career counselors have short exercises, checklists, or tests that can be completed in an hour or less, which may point out some general directions. A discussion with a qualified counselor and/or the completion of such exercises may result in a tentative emergency decision. However, this should be viewed as a temporary measure only! While it may be true that more comprehensive career development activities later will verify the general direction that you arrived at as a result of the above emergency efforts, it does not negate the need to engage in more comprehensive career development. While such "Band-Aid" measures are often required to meet the sometimes overwhelming demands of a fast-moving society, the most successful professionals will strongly recommend follow-up activities.

17 What is an MBA?

MBA stands for master's of business administration. Traditionally, the acquisition of an MBA, particularly if it has been earned at one of the nation's top business schools (e.g., Harvard, Michigan, Stanford) signifies that one has been well-educated and is highly qualified to step into the world of business. For years, MBA candidates, as well as many professionals, have regarded this degree as the one to acquire if you expect to succeed in corporate America. The MBA has been touted as the key to higher salaries and upper-level executive positions. Indeed, some would probably say that the MBA is to business what the Ph.D. is to college teaching. However, several years ago, some began to question these lofty perceptions. Some of these questions came out of concerns about how adequately many business schools were keeping pace with the times. Additional questions were asked about the quality of America's business schools. At the time, some believed this was due to a weakened posture American business had been forced to take because of stiff global competition. Other reasons cited included the infusion of new technologies and changing management techniques. Nevertheless, the MBA remains a cherished goal for most aspiring business students and still appears to carry considerable weight in the business community (particularly if it comes from an Ivy League school).

18 Should I go for an MBA?

This is probably a question that is asked by most, if not all, undergraduate business majors. Before you make a decision, carefully consider the following:

- **Age.** Do you believe that the years you will have to benefit from acquiring the MBA will outweigh the projected time and effort required to earn it?
- **Cost.** Will you be able to recoup the expenses incurred from attending an MBA program for several years?
- **Values and Family Lifestyle.** Will the pursuit of an MBA, as well as projected benefits later on, be supportive of your desired values and lifestyle?

The following is a brief summary of pros and cons of pursuing an MBA:

Pros

- MBA's usually enjoy a higher salary than non-MBA's.
- In larger corporations, an MBA may improve your chances for advancement and promotion.
- MBA programs usually involve a broad-based (often including an international aspect) and future-directed perspective, which is greatly needed in an increasingly competitive and global market.
- The MBA saves job candidates the frustration of being passed over because of a lack of credentials.
- The MBA is still viewed by many as "desirable" and may provide opportunities in unrelated areas.

Cons

- Some employers shy away from MBA grads, believing that they are overrated, lack technical skills, expect salaries higher than they are willing to pay, and that they may quickly move on to another company.
- An MBA program can be very expensive, possibly costing as much as two years of lost salary—which may never be recouped.
- The pursuit of an MBA may place a significant strain on family time and finances.

- Some may find out after completion of an MBA program that the sacrifice was not required, particularly those who either start their own businesses or remain in smaller ones.
- If your MBA is not earned from one of the nation's top business schools, you may experience difficulty in landing the type of position you desire.
- You may have unrealistic expectations regarding what the MBA will do for you once acquired.

19 Should I get a PH.D.?

Whether you should go for the Ph.D. (Doctor of Philosophy)—or for that matter, any graduate degree—depends on how you answer the following types of questions:

- Do the values, lifestyle, and occupation I am seeking require that I go on to graduate school?
- Do I have and/or can I afford the expense of going on to graduate school?
- Will the outlay of money, time, and energy be worth the expected benefits later on?
- Am I willing to do the rigorous and time-consuming research usually required for the final dissertation?
- Do I have to work while I pursue this degree or can I quit work and attend school full-time?
- What is the likelihood I will get a job related to my studies?
- Will the pursuit of a Ph.D. come into severe conflict with my other life values, particularly concerning my family?

These questions should be answered by the potential Ph.D. candidate prior to starting a program of study. A thorough self-analysis should be the first priority. If the results clearly point to areas such as university teaching, higher education administration, research, computer science, or engineering supervision, then a Ph.D. should be a definite consideration. In order to obtain the highest level professional jobs in mathematics, physics, psychology, sociology, engineering, and many other academic disciplines, a Ph.D. is required. The Ph.D. might also be your goal if you have a continuing desire to learn and be intellectually stimulated through research, discovery, and publishing. Others may choose this route in order to obtain the status and job advantages often associated with the Ph.D. However, some may want to avoid such a rigorous academic endeavor if they dislike or are weak in the areas of language, writing, and research. Listed below are some of the pros and cons of pursuing a Ph.D.

Pros
- May open up many more professional and/or supervisory employment possibilities.
- Increased prestige and status; you may be considered an expert in your area.

- Opportunity to earn more income.
- Usually increases one's credibility in terms of published materials, etc.
- Will probably put you in a good position to take advantage of an increasingly complex and knowledge-oriented society in terms of being able to apply skills learned.
- Having the satisfaction of learning at a highly specialized level.

Cons

- A great deal of time is normally required. (It is estimated that the average candidate takes about six or seven years beyond the bachelor's degree to complete the Ph.D.)
- After receiving a Ph.D., and if employed in a university setting, you may be pressured to "publish or perish."
- The cost of obtaining a Ph.D. can be very expensive.
- May experience discrimination from some employers who consider you overqualified.
- The written dissertation is a major obstacle for many.
- Some may not be able to find the most desired employment and thus may experience underemployment.

Finally, if you are seriously considering the pursuit of a Ph.D., be sure to get input from postdoctoral and current graduate students in your area of interest before making a decision.

20 What is an apprenticeship?

An apprenticeship is an arrangement between an employer and an individual (referred to as an apprentice) whereby the apprentice agrees to be trained and supervised by a skilled craftsperson(s) for a specified period of time. Apprenticeship experiences combine classroom instruction and on-the-job training, which must add up to a minimum number of required hours (usually around 8,000 hours or four years of on-the-job experience and a minimum of 576 hours of related instruction). During this time, the apprentice is paid at a progressively higher rate of pay. If the apprenticeship is successfully completed, the apprentice usually applies for and receives his or her Journey Worker's Card, which represents full status as a skilled craftsperson in a particular area of training. (However, be aware that one may acquire a Journey Worker's Card, usually via a union, and not have completed an official apprenticeship program.)

Some occupations that offer apprenticeship training include: Automobile-Body Repairer, Electronics Mechanic, Automobile Mechanic, Emergency Medical Technician, Baker, Firefighter, Biomedical Equipment Technician, Furniture Finisher, Boilermaker, Glazier, Butcher, Hazardous Waste Material Technician, Bricklayer, Instrument Mechanic, Cabinetmaker, Legal Secretary, Carpenter,

Machinist, Cement Mason, Millwright, Cosmetologist, Painter, Drafter, Plumber, Electrician, Sheet-Metal Worker.

21 What is co-op education?

Co-op (short for cooperative) education is a joint venture between an educational institution and an employer to provide a learning experience for one or more students, combining classroom studies with related on-the-job work activities. Normally, the student is paid and the work experience is supervised by representatives from both of the parties involved. Co-op programs are widespread and are administered through many high school, college, and university job placement offices or business departments. The co-op student may spend part of his or her day or semester on the job while the other part is spent in the classroom. In some cases, students rotate between terms of full-time study and terms of full-time work. Many co-op programs grant academic credits.

Pros
- May lead to job with the employer
- Prepares student for "real world" due to large block of time required for work
- Can earn money for school fees and other expenses
- Can help determine career direction
- Experience can enhance your resume and interviews
- Develops work experiences/contacts
- Can enrich one's personal development

Cons
- May not be able to take other academic courses
- May find out that area is not suited for you and thus waste valuable time and energy
- May not be able to participate in as many school-related or campus activities due to full schedule

22 What are home study courses?

Traditionally, home study courses (sometimes referred to as correspondence courses or "taking courses at a distance") have been off-campus courses taken by individuals via mail. However, the mode of delivery has changed dramatically due to advanced technology. A wide range of classes can be taken via the correspondence route, from elementary through the graduate level. Correspondence courses can be particularly attractive to those who are shut-in. John Bear's book entitled *College Degree by Mail or Modem* (Ten Speed Press, 1999) comprehensively covers this topic.

Pros

- Provides one-on-one teaching experience
- Flexible and convenient with faculty, students, etc.
- Can work at one's own pace .
- Can usually enroll at any time
- Can experience personal growth and satisfaction from achievements
- Can save time and money (transportation, clothes, etc.)
- No scheduling hassles

Cons

- Reduced "in person" interactions
- Need for strong self-discipline
- Distractions at home
- May not be able to transfer courses to a traditional program later
- Increased isolation

23 What is virtual education?

Virtual education can be considered an outgrowth of distance learning, resulting from widespread technological advances. In essence, it is taking academic and/or training classes electronically (primarily via the computer) instead of in an educational institution.

This form of educational training is growing rapidly. Sam Atieh has written a book about such opportunities entitled *How to Get a College Degree via the Internet* (Prima Publishing, 1998). Various technologies are utilized, although the computer is the primary tool. Depending upon the school, program, and class, other methods or technologies used may include interactive TV; computer conferencing; audiographics; audiocassettes; telecourses; videotape courses; email; teleconferencing; and fax machines. Some colleges offer entire programs of study virtually. And students at more and more of these "virtual colleges" can access libraries around the world virtually.

For more information, contact the U.S. Distance Learning Association (USDLA) at http://www.usdla.org/

24 What is an internship?

An internship is an experience offering an individual an opportunity to work in a real job situation for a prescribed period of time to gain knowledge, skills, and work experience. Internships are usually related to one's area of study and can be engaged in with or without financial compensation or other work benefits. While many internships take place during the summer months, in areas such as teaching, they may take place anytime during the year and last for a much longer period of time. Some professional internships last a year or more. A growing number of college programs now require the successful completion of an internship before a certificate or degree is granted. Some internships offer academic credits.

Pros

- Can learn job-holding behaviors
- Can establish contacts for future employment
- Can help in making career decisions
- Can gain experience valuable on resumes and in interviews

Cons

- May offer reduced or no pay
- May take time away from paid work experience
- May find during the internship that the area is not for you and thus waste valuable time and energy

25 What is mentoring?

Mentoring occurs when an experienced and/or skilled adult (often in an influential leadership position) takes another individual (or mentoree) who is less experienced, knowledgeable, and skilled, under his or her wing, for the purpose of:

1. Instructing, coaching, and advising in order to help the mentoree overcome potential obstacles and increase the chances for career success;

2. Sharing important "inside information" about a company, organization, agency, or institution; or

3. Being a contact and support person as well as an advocate for the mentoree in terms of future employment possibilities or promotions.

Having a mentor appears to be extremely advantageous for a growing number who seek to get a foot in the door and learn what it takes to experience upward career mobility within a particular organization. But mentoring relationships have both pros and cons:

Pros

- Increased chance to be noticed and thus permanently employed or promoted
- Opportunity to learn from the inside of a company
- Can pick up skills of use in other situations
- Can acquire valuable tips to prevent mistakes later
- Can cut down on the amount of time one needs to move up
- Can build a support base

Cons

- Danger of becoming too intimate with or dependent on mentor
- May create friction among mentor's co-workers
- Advice by mentor may come into conflict with others
- May be perceived as a threat by some

- May be unfairly used by mentor
- If the experience doesn't turn out well, may hamper your prospects at the company

26 What is networking and can it help me?

Networking is simply establishing as many relevant personal contacts as possible in order to enhance future career possibilities and personal growth. This could include a wide range of individuals, from family members, friends, and job/school associates to professional acquaintances developed at conventions and meetings and through referrals. Most people engage in networking whether they realize it or not—through discussions about mutual interests, fellowship, and other interchanges. Networking is viewed negatively by some people because they feel the individual who seeks to network may selfishly take advantage of others. Unfortunately, this may be true of some. However, networking can and should be a give-and-take arrangement wherein both persons involved derive benefit from the interaction and each assists the other.

27 What are "high-tech" jobs?

According to the U.S. Department of Labor, high-tech jobs represent one of the fastest growing occupational areas in the country. These jobs, while only a small percentage of the labor force, continue to increase. Most of us probably associate high-tech with computers, robotics, and automated processes, but there is some difference of opinion as to really what constitutes a high-tech job. We like the definition used by the Department of Labor, which says that high-tech jobs are characterized by:

- A significant number of workers (higher than the average) within the occupation considered scientific or technical employees
- The allocation of monies (more than the average occupation) for research and development
- Workers with a good command of the theories and principles of mathematics, science, and engineering

While there are numerous jobs that fit the above criteria, some of the more common ones are computer analysts, engineers, and technicians; science technicians; physical scientists; engineers and engineering technicians; and mathematicians.

28 How do I know if a program or institution is good?

While in some instances this may require considerable investigation, a general evaluation of an academic/training program or institution can be obtained by checking its accreditation status. Most college directories, such as Peterson's guides, include accreditation status. Accreditation procedures are usually thorough and comprehensive and normally include on-site observations and periodical evaluations. To obtain accreditation, an institution or program has to meet previously determined acceptable standards of quality, a few of which appear below.

- Academic performance of students
- Competence level of the faculty and administration (amount of training, degrees earned, recognitions, etc.)
- Appropriateness of curriculum
- Quality of library and technology resources
- Quality of student support services (such as disabled student assistance, tutoring, career development and job placement services, foreign student support, and student activities)
- Adequacy of physical facilities

In addition, you can evaluate a program or institution by:

- Seeing how closely it complements your personality attributes and helps you to realize your fundamental life values (you can determine this with a self-assessment or by consulting a career counselor)
- Obtaining a sampling of opinions from current and past students and instructors
- Checking the institution's job placement records (ask how many of the recent graduates in your interest area are employed in related fields)
- Ascertaining the institution's public image and credibility (in other words, what do professionals in your community, past and present students, friends, and community residents say about it?)
- Taking note of the ratio of applicants accepted to students enrolled

29 What is a liberal arts major?

A liberal arts major refers to a concentration of courses in nontechnical, nonspecialized areas such as anthropology, art, foreign language, political science, communications, literature, religion, English, history, music, economics, journalism, philosophy, psychology, and sociology.

Students who have successfully completed liberal arts curricula normally demonstrate proficiencies in many, if not most, of the following knowledge and skill areas, which are important for occupational flexibility, advancement, and overall life fulfillment:

- Ability to analyze and synthesize information
- Critical thinking and reasoning ability
- Ability to read analytically and speak articulately
- Active listening
- Ability to make good judgments and keen observations
- Ability to solve problems and apply the steps of good decision-making
- Interpersonal communication
- Tolerance for change and ambiguity

- Understanding underlying causes and ability to see the "big picture"
- Self-discipline and good organizational skills
- Flexibility
- Appreciation for diversity
- Identifying trends and implications
- Ability to get along with people of different racial and ethnic backgrounds and personalities

30 What are career tests?

It may help to first define test. Any procedure that attempts to measure or evaluate in order to determine quality, achievement, or ability level, can be said to be a test. Career tests are actually surveys, in that they attempt to help you to identify interests, skills, and various personality characteristics in order to help you to make appropriate career-related decisions.

31 Should the results of my career tests determine what I do in the future?

Absolutely not! This is an incorrect assumption that is believed by people far too often. Career tests results should only verify other information you have obtained about yourself so that a better and more informed decision can be made. The intricately complex nature of the human being as well as the highly technical and changing society we live in can never be fully measured by human-devised evaluations. However, when the appropriate career or aptitude test is used, it can be highly beneficial.

Even if it were possible to determine precisely what you should do in the future, it is probably more important to answer the following questions: Are my career interests or aptitude test results generally supportive of my most cherished life values? Do the results complement my personality attributes? Do the results provide me with enough additional information and insight to help me to make a better decision about my career direction? Once again, the most important thing to remember is to combine the results of any career assessment you take with as much additional information as you need to be able to make an informed and wise decision.

32 Should I accept career test results that point to a single field?

Possibly, although you should not act too hastily, even if the results seem to verify your career focus. Also, if you have not had a qualified career counselor assist you in your interpretation, I would strongly encourage you to do so. It is usually wise to have several indicators clearly point in the same direction. I would recommend three to five verifications of direction (e.g., career survey results, favorite school courses and/or those in which you have the highest grades, career worksheet results, feedback from credible others, your own personal beliefs, etc.). Multiple verifications usually minimize the tendency for one to doubt or have continuing second thoughts. They should increase your confidence as well as the chances for you to realize personal satisfaction in life. Finally, using several clear indicators may help you to avoid spending time, effort, and money moving in an inappropriate direction.

33 What does it mean when the results of my career testing show that I am interested in just about everything?

While there are a number of possible reasons for such a profile, it is more than likely that one or more of the following is true:

- You may have purposely put down answers which would show a high interest in everything so as not to miss out on anything exciting or interesting.
- You have broad and strong interests in many different areas but may not know enough about yourself to identify those areas which represent the highest priority.
- You lack decision-making skills.
- You simply marked all of the items "favorable" in order to just get through.
- You genuinely have strong interests in many areas, but, unrealistically, want to do everything.
- You may have misunderstood or responded incorrectly.
- There may have been a mechanical (or computer) malfunction or a human recording error.

In such cases, if you cannot identify the reason (and eventually resolve your confusion) from among the above possibilities, it is suggested that you seek the help of a qualified career counselor or do what you most want to do (given that other verifications support the decision).

34 Am I required to take a battery of tests to effectively plan my career?

No. There are a number of resources that can help you to determine career direction. Some people, because of family influences, their past experiences with counselors, and other career-directing activities, have developed a clear understanding of themselves and their values. Certain individuals have been fortunate to have had interested and knowledgeable teachers who continuously encouraged them in self-analysis, exploration, and good decision-making or maybe a mother or uncle just happened to be a career counselor. Still others have benefited from a variety of career-oriented family visitors or comprehensive home libraries or enriching trips and vacations. Consequently, they not only continually monitor change within and around themselves continually, but they have learned effective decision-making skills.

Some find the results of career-related worksheets, exercises, and written questionnaires sufficient to make appropriate career decisions. Others simply develop, over time, the necessary motivation and direction by reading books and other publications and doing Internet research. Finally, certain individuals develop an effective system of career decision-making through career-oriented audiovisuals; seminars, workshops, and conferences; clubs; classroom and community lectures and discussions; computer software programs; work, volunteer, co-op, or internship experiences; and talking to others.

As you can see, career tests represent only one of a variety of career development activities for you to consider. Testing may not be required or even appropriate for you due to time constraints, cost, language difficulty, reading level, or availability, just to name a few reasons. However, you will want to be absolutely sure you have enough information about yourself and the world around you to better ensure that you are making wise career decisions.

35 What is the difference between an aptitude test and an interest inventory?

While these two types of tests attempt to measure something quite different, I have found that many individuals do not know the difference and are confused. A frequently heard statement is, "I'd like to take one of those aptitude tests." This statement could be referring to an occupational interest inventory, abilities test, or a personality survey. Quite often, after some clarifying questions, it is discovered that the individual actually desired a more comprehensive test to help him or her make a better decision.

Aptitude Tests—according to Harcourt Brace Jovanovich, Inc., publishers of the popular Differential Aptitude Tests (DAT), aptitude is "the capacity to learn given appropriate training and environmental input." Aptitudes are considered by this leading test publisher as learned and not inherited. Its tests attempt to measure one's degree of "readiness or potential to perform or do" in some identified area(s). An aptitude test seeks to establish if one has a strong, average, or weak tendency to perform well, based on natural and/or learned abilities in selected areas (e.g., spatial, verbal, numerical, mechanical, abstract reasoning, clerical, etc.). Normally, the results of an aptitude test do not provide enough diagnostic information for those seeking to establish career direction, unless they are added to other relevant data.

Interest Inventories (Surveys)—These tests are widely used and may be mistakenly perceived by some as having more comprehensive career development application than they have been designed for. Interest inventories attempt to identify significant trends toward or away from selected occupational areas, the objective being to compare the inventory-taker's interests with the general interests of individuals in designated occupations. Interest inventories are based on the premise that the more one's interests are like/unlike individuals in selected occupations, the more compatible/incompatible the occupational area is likely to be. Nevertheless, just as it is true for aptitude tests, interest inventory results are limited, no matter how accurate, and represent only one of a number of important aspects which should be considered in career decision-making.

36 Should I "test out" of a required course?

It depends on your particular circumstance, but it may be to your advantage to test out if one or more of the following is true:

- You are thoroughly proficient in the basic knowledge and/or skills that will be covered in the course; to take the course would be a rehash of what you already know and thus may be a waste of valuable time. For example, if you've been a freelance writer for five years, testing out of a basic composition course in your degree program makes good sense.
- Extenuating circumstances—such as disabilities—that keep you from taking on-campus courses, or serious time conflicts due to family or job obligations demand that an alternative to regular classroom attendance be explored.
- You have taken an advanced placement (AP) class during high school in the area you want to test out of and you are quite knowledgeable and/or highly capable in that area. In this instance, testing out may allow you to move into advanced courses and thus shorten the time required to earn your degree, Remember, the rationale here for testing out is that you are already highly capable. If this is not true, then maybe taking the course would be the wiser choice. If in doubt, see a qualified counselor.

On the other hand, testing out may not be the best option if one or more of the following reflects your present situation.

- Due to a lack of effort, knowledge, or ability, you have failed a required course and thus would like to test out of it to avoid taking it over again.
- You believe you can pass the test and are looking for a quick and easy way to obtain a degree. Not only is there a good chance you will not pass, but you may very well find out later that you have unnecessarily shortchanged yourself, in terms of the enriching educational experiences that often result from classroom exposure.
- The course is in an important foundation area that will give you knowledge and skills you will later need to apply regularly and with significant proficiency. In such instances, it is recommended that you take the actual class. It is unlikely that a test will be able to duplicate the formal and informal discussions between instructor and student that a classroom experience affords. A great deal of learning—as well as valuable networking opportunities—can be lost if one is not exposed to such experiences. To test out of courses that demand depth and breadth in all aspects could eventually put you at a disadvantage in the future.

Those interested in testing out should contact their high school or college counselor and ask about Advanced Placement, CLEP Tests, GED Tests, and/or any Challenge Tests (faculty-made) that may be available.

37 Can occupational projections be trusted?

Some would answer, "Well, yes!" and others would say, "Probably not." Whatever position you take, it must be clearly understood that occupational projections are merely educated guesses, though they may be based on extensive research. No human being can foretell the future perfectly; many variables can and do, often unexpectedly, affect outcomes (e.g., supply and demand, technological advances, weather, war, etc.). Predictions have often been known not to hold up. Nevertheless, job projections can be quite helpful when coupled with other related data, particularly if information is obtained from a reliable source. A key resource, considered to be credible by most, is the U.S. Bureau of Labor Statistics (BLS), a governmental agency that specializes in occupational predictions. Many college and university career development and placement centers, as well as state employment service offices, maintain a file of updated labor market projections from the BLS and other sources. Also, many career specialists believe that jobs are available in most occupational areas, regardless of job predictions. However, to acquire these jobs, an individual must learn and effectively implement the skills of job hunting (including via the Internet) and self-marketing. I am inclined to agree.

38 What are some common problems that often hamper career development?

There is a limitless number of obstacles that can seriously jeopardize career progress. The following represent some of those frequently voiced by our clients over the years. For most we have included some general suggestions on how one can begin to overcome such obstacles. In addition, several positive qualities that might develop, should the obstacle be overcome, have been cited in some instances. Finally, a suggested resource may be included for a few of the obstacles listed. However, it is strongly recommended that if any of the problems below persist, please seek the help of a qualified professional. Suggestions are provided as starting points only.

- **Procrastination**—An ex-procrastinator could become one who is thorough, analytical, and cautious before acting. A helpful little booklet published by Pathway Books is James R. Sherman's *Do It*.
- **Work-Family Conflict**—Effectively coping with conflicts arising between work and family can help one to develop time-management, self-discipline, and conflict management skills. Several books on the topic are available and individual counseling can be helpful.

- **Lack of Information, Education, or Training**—Conduct a thorough self-assessment and engage in related career development activities; read career materials and talk to people in your area of interest; if necessary, enroll into a related course of study. Those who lack information, education, or training can develop self-confidence and the ability to sift through unnecessary information and thus avoid a significant waste of time, money, and energy. See a qualified professional counselor.
- **Financial Need**—Always explore financial aid options and consider going to school part-time, attending a community college, or taking courses through correspondence programs.
- **Perfectionism**—With professional counseling, a former perfectionist can develop into one who is neat, exact, precise, and thorough.
- **Lack of Self-Confidence**—Very often, if you obtain knowledge about yourself and what you want in life, along with information about acquiring a more fulfilling life, it will serve to build confidence (particularly if you also develop new skills). Minimize or eliminate negative images of yourself; realistically list accomplishments, no matter how small they may appear; associate with those who encourage rather than discourage you. A person who formerly lacked self-confidence may develop into one who is conscientious, reliable, and encouraging to others.
- **Indecisive**—Conduct a thorough self-assessment and engage in related career development activities; learn and apply the steps of good decision-making. A person who formerly made haphazard and generally poor decisions may develop the qualities of patience, courage, and wisdom (particularly with the assistance of a qualified career counselor).
- **Stress**—Often characterized by frustration, fear, and general discomfort due to conflicts in relationships, time, responsibilities, and values, some possible solutions include physical exercise, recreation, rest, self-assessment identification and implementation, and time management. Very often, college counseling and career centers, as well as women's resource centers, distribute materials on this topic.

Appendix A
Descriptions of Selected Occupations

The following descriptions should encompass the least familiar occupations mentioned in this book. Most of the occupational definitions cited are based to some extent on information provided in the *Dictionary of Occupational Titles* (DOT) and the *Occupational Outlook Handbook*. For a comprehensive and detailed list of occupational definitions, consult the latest edition of the DOT.

ABSTRACTOR—A worker who analyzes pertinent legal or insurance details or sections of statute or case law to summarize for purposes of examination, proof, or ready reference—may specialize as a title examiner.

ACCOUNTING CLERK—A clerical worker who performs any combination of routine calculating, posting, and verifying of financial information for use in maintaining accounting records.

ACQUISITIONS LIBRARIAN—A librarian who selects and orders books, periodicals, films, and other materials for a library.

ACTIVITIES SUPERVISOR—A recreation therapist who specializes in the organization, direction, and supervision of recreational activities for those individuals who are elderly, ill, or disabled to assist in their overall rehabilitation.

ACTUARY—A professional who applies knowledge of mathematics, probability, statistics, and principles of finance and business to various forms of insurance, annuities, and pensions.

ADJUDICATOR—A government worker who adjudicates (gives an opinion on) claims filed by the government against individuals or organizations.

ADMINISTRATIVE EXAMINER—A worker who supervises and oversees polygraph examiners who question and screen individuals to detect deception or to verify truthfulness using polygraph equipment and techniques.

ADMIRALTY LAWYER—A lawyer who specializes in legal matters pertaining to inland navigable waters or on the high seas.

ADULT AND VOCATIONAL EDUCATION TEACHER—A teacher who specializes in preparing students for a particular vocation such as welding, food service, or horticulture.

ADVERTISING ACCOUNT EXECUTIVE—A professional who plans, coordinates, and directs advertising campaigns for the clients of an advertising agency.

AERODYNAMIST—An engineering specialist who plans and conducts the analyses of aerodynamic, thermodynamic, aerothermodynamic, and aerophysics concepts, systems, and designs to resolve problems and determine suitability and application to aircraft and spacecraft.

AERONAUTICAL ENGINEER—An engineer who applies engineering principles and techniques to design, develop, and test aircraft, space vehicles, surface effect vehicles, and missiles.

AEROSPACE ENGINEER—An engineer who designs, develops, tests, and helps produce commercial and military aircraft, missiles, and spacecraft.

ARCHIVIST—A professional who appraises and organizes permanent records and historically valuable documents, participates in research activities involving archival materials, and directs the safekeeping of archival documents and materials.

ART THERAPIST—A health care specialist who plans, coordinates, and supervises art techniques, projects, and programs to assist in the rehabilitation of mentally or physically challenged patients.

ASTROPHYSICIST—A physicist who specializes in the study of the physical aspects of the heavenly bodies or space such as the sun, stars, and planets.

AUDIOLOGIST—A professional therapist who specializes in diagnostic evaluation of hearing, prevention research, and habilitative services for hearing problems and related disorders.

AUDITOR—An accounting professional who examines or audits financial records and controls operating procedures to determine effectiveness and efficiency—may specialize in internal, external, county, tax, or other kinds of auditing.

BACTERIOLOGIST—See Microbiologist.

BAILIFF—A court officer who maintains order in a courtroom during trials and guards the jury from outside contact—can arrest persons violating the law and is responsible for overall security.

BAR EXAMINER—A professional who determines the qualifications of candidates seeking to practice law—prepares written exams, corrects and marks papers, announces those who pass, and makes recommendations.

BIBLIOGRAPHER—A professional who compiles lists of books, periodicals, articles, and audiovisual materials on specialized subjects.

BIOCHEMIST—A professional scientist who studies chemical processes of living organisms and conducts research to determine the influence of foods, drugs, serums, and other substances on tissues and vital processes.

BIOMEDICAL ENGINEER—An engineer who specializes in using medical and biological ideas and principles in the design, development, production, and supervision of medical equipment and devices.

BIOMEDICAL EQUIPMENT TECHNICIAN—A worker who specializes in the inspection, maintenance, calibration, and modification of the electronic, electrical, mechanical, hydraulic, and pneumatic equipment and instruments used in medical therapy.

BIOPHYSICIST—A biological scientist who studies the physical principles of living cells and organisms, their electrical and mechanical energy, and related phenomena.

BIOSTATISTICIAN—See Statistician.

BLACKSMITH—A worker who creates and repairs various metal articles such as tongs, edged tools, hooks, chains, machine and structural components, and agricultural articles.

BLOOD BANK SPECIALIST—A health care worker who specializes in both simple and advanced blood techniques such as drawing blood, classification, collection and transfusion, testing, evaluation, preservation and storage, and other related activities.

BOILERMAKER—A worker who assembles, analyzes defects in, and repairs boilers, pressure vessels, tanks, and vats using power and hand tools.

BOOKBINDER—A worker who cuts, sews, and glues the pages of a book to its cover, using a sewing machine, hand press, and hand cutter.

BOTANIST—A biological scientist who studies the development and life processes, physiology, heredity, environment, distribution, anatomy, morphology, and economic value of plants for application in such fields as agronomy, forestry, horticulture, and pharmacology.

BUYER—A professional who purchases merchandise or commodities for resale, inspecting, selecting, ordering, and authorizing payment for them.

CABLE SPLICER—A worker who splices overhead, underground, or submarine multiple-conductor cables used in telephone and telegraph communications and electric power transmission systems.

CARDIOLOGIST—A medical doctor who specializes in the diagnosis, treatment, and prevention of diseases of the heart.

CARTOGRAPHER—A professional drafter who specializes in drawing maps of geographical areas to show natural and constructed features, political boundaries, and other features.

CATALOGER—A librarian who compiles information and materials such as books and periodicals and prepares catalog cards to identify materials and integrate information into a library's collection.

CATERER—One who coordinates the food service activities of a hotel, restaurant, or other similar establishment or at a social function—includes food preparation, budgeting, menu planning, managing staff, and maintaining food quality.

CERAMIC ENGINEER—An engineer who specializes in developing new nonmetallic, inorganic materials and new methods for making ceramic materials into useable products.

CHAMBER OF COMMERCE OFFICER—One who represents a local association of businesspeople who aim to promote commercial and industrial interests in the community—involves analyzing of market trends, economic conditions, and tax issues; advising businesses; supporting economic and civic growth; and other activities.

CHAPLAIN—A clergy worker who conducts and coordinates worship services, evangelism activities, and religious education endeavors in the armed forces, correctional institutions, hospitals, and on college campuses.

CHEMICAL LABORATORY TECHNICIAN—A worker who conducts chemical and physical laboratory tests and makes qualitative and quantitative analyses of materials, liquids, and gases for the purpose of research, new products, health and safety standards, criminology, environmental concerns, and more.

CHIEF EXECUTIVE OFFICER (CEO)—The top executive or administrator of a large corporation or government.

CHILD WELFARE WORKER—A social worker (caseworker) who aids parents with child-rearing problems and children who have difficulties in social adjustments; investigates home conditions; refers clients to community resources; coordinates foster care or adoption activities; provides counsel to families; and supervises and monitors placements.

CHIROPRACTOR—A physician, but not a medical doctor, who specializes in the adjustment of the spinal column and other body parts to improve health and correct abnormalities of the human body believed to be caused by interferences with the nervous system.

CHOREOGRAPHER—A dance director who creates and teaches original dances for ballet, musical, or revue to be performed for stage, TV, motion picture, or nightclub production.

CINEMATOGRAPHER—A photography director who plans, directs, and coordinates the filming of a motion picture.

CIRCULATION MANAGER—A manager who directs the sales and distribution of newspapers, books, and periodicals.

CITY MANAGER—A government administrator who directs and coordinates the administration of a city or county government in accordance with policies determined by a city council or other authorized officials.

CIVIL ENGINEER—An engineer who plans, designs, and directs the construction and maintenance of structures and facilities such as roads, railroads, airports, bridges, harbors, channels, dams, irrigation projects, pipelines, power plants, water and sewage systems, and waste disposal units.

CLIMATOLOGIST—A meteorologist who specializes in the study of climate and climatic conditions.

CLINICAL CHEMIST—A biochemist who studies the chemical processes of living organisms and uses complex chemical tests and procedures to analyze body tissues and fluids.

COAL PIPELINE OPERATOR—A worker who controls, from a master panel, a semiautomatic processing plant that pulverizes and mixes coal with water and sends the resulting slurry into a pipeline for transportation.

COLLEGE ADMINISTRATIVE DEAN—A college administrator who directs and coordinates a specific area of responsibility such as student affairs, academics, occupational programs, continuing education, men, or women.

COLUMNIST—An individual who analyzes news and writes a column or commentary based on personal knowledge and experience with the subject matter for publication or broadcast

COMMERCIAL ARTIST —A professional artist who draws or paints illustrations for use by various media to explain or enhance the printed or spoken word.

COMMUNITY SERVICE AGENCY DIRECTOR—An individual who directs the activities of a community health or social service agency concerned with community problems such as teen pregnancy, child abuse, substance abuse, or disease.

COMPOSITOR—A worker who assembles and sets type by hand or machine and creates galleys for printed materials.

COMPUTER SECURITY SPECIALIST—An individual who evaluates the security of computer systems; also trained to prevent, safeguard against, and investigate computer-related crimes.

CONSERVATIONIST—A worker who is concerned with the protection and care of natural resources such as streams, rivers, lakes, and forests.

CONSULTANT—A professional who has developed a proficiency or expertise in a particular area and is consulted by clients to define a need or problem, conduct studies or surveys to obtain information, and analyze data to give advice on or recommend a solution.

CONTRACTOR—A manager who contracts to perform specified construction work in accordance with architectural plans, blueprints, and codes—may be classified as a building contractor, landscape contractor, engineering contractor, or other specialized contractor.

CONTROLLER/COMPTROLLER—An individual who directs the financial affairs of an organization such as a bank, hospital, governmental office, or hotel.

COOPERATIVE EXTENSION WORKER—An agricultural agent who organizes meetings to advise farmers and individuals engaged in agribusiness in application of agricultural research findings; may direct 4-H club activities, give lectures, and prepare articles—sometimes called an agricultural extension agent.

COPYWRITER—A professional who writes or revises material (copy) for use by print or broadcast media to promote the sale of goods and services.

CORONER—A medical examiner who directs investigations of death occurring within a particular jurisdiction as required by law. Coroners conduct inquests, perform autopsies and laboratory analyses, and may testify at hearings or trials.

CORRECTIONS OFFICER—An individual who is responsible for guarding inmates in jails and prisons in accordance with established policies, regulations, and procedures.

COUNTY PROSECUTOR—See District Attorney.

COURT REPORTER—A clerk who performs clerical duties in a court of law, including preparing a calendar of cases, examining legal documents, explaining procedures, securing information, recording minutes of court proceedings, and other tasks.

CREDIT MANAGER—A worker who directs and coordinates the activities of a federal or state chartered credit union that provides savings and loans services to members.

CRIMINOLOGIST—A professional sociologist who specializes in the study of crime and criminal behavior.

CURATOR—A professional who oversees the collection, research, authentication, preservation, maintenance, and information dissemination activities of operating and exhibiting institutions such as museums, botanical gardens, arboretums, art galleries, herbariums, and zoos.

CURRICULUM SUPERVISOR—A professional educator who supervises and oversees the implementation of an instructional materials program in an elementary, junior high, or high school in accordance with guidelines.

CUSTOMS INSPECTOR—A government worker who inspects cargo, baggage, and articles worn or carried by persons on vessels, vehicles, or aircraft entering or leaving the country to enforce customs and related laws.

CYTOLOGIST—A biological scientist who studies plant or animal cells.

CYTOTECHNOLOGIST—A health care specialist who assists pathologists through the process of staining, mounting, and studying cells of the human body to determine pathological conditions.

DANCE THERAPIST—A specialist who plans, organizes, and directs dance activities and learning experiences as part of the care and treatment of patients to produce positive behavioral changes.

DATABASE MANAGER—A worker who supervises and manages the designing, creating, and operating activities in the formulation of a computerized information storage bank.

DATA ENTRY EQUIPMENT OPERATOR—A worker who enters information into a computer system.

DENTAL HYGIENIST—A health care worker who specializes in removing plaque and tartar from teeth and beneath the gumline; also does preliminary examinations for the dentist.

DENTAL LAB TECHNICIAN—A health care worker who builds and repairs full and partial dentures (sets of teeth), bridges, crowns, and other dental apparatuses using hand tools, molding equipment, and bench fabricating machines.

DERMATOLOGIST—A medical doctor who specializes in the diagnosis and treatment of diseases and conditions of the skin.

DESIGN/BUILDING SPECIALIST—An architect who specializes in both the design and physical building aspect of a project; may work with a contractor or make modifications on his or her own.

DESKTOP PUBLISHER—A professional who produces printed materials via computer using the techniques of layout and graphic design.

DIAGNOSTIC MEDICAL SONOGRAPHER—A health care specialist who utilizes ultrasound diagnostic procedures, which make use of sonic energy to identify or determine the extent of disease or injury in body tissue.

DIETETIC TECHNICIAN—A worker under the direction of a dietitian who assists in food service management, nutrition education, and dietary counseling.

DIETITIAN—A health care specialist who directs, plans, and supervises programs for menu planning, food preparation, nutritional care, serving of meals, and specialized diets.

DIPLOMAT—See Foreign Service Officer.

DIRECTOR OF ADMISSIONS—A professional who directs and coordinates a student admissions program at private schools or public and private colleges or universities according to policies developed by a governing board; determines who will be accepted; prepares and distributes materials about the institution and its programs; and conducts recruitment programs.

DIRECTOR OF CAREER PLACEMENT—A professional who directs and supervises job placement services for students and employees—usually arranges for interviews, posts or publicizes listings of job openings, supervises and coordinates campus work-study programs, offers seminars and workshops related to job seeking-holding skills, develops and distributes occupational information, etc.

DIRECTOR OF GUIDANCE—A professional counseling administrator who directs and coordinates educational and vocational guidance and counseling programs for students and graduates.

DISPATCHER—A worker who dispatches buses, cabs, trains, airplanes, trucks, and other transporting vehicles; supervises, coordinates, and relays schedules and instructions regarding movement and location; also maintains an operational log.

DISTRICT ATTORNEY—A lawyer who conducts prosecutions in court proceedings on behalf of the city, county, state, or federal government; presents evidence against the accused to a grand jury and before a judge or other judiciary or jury.

DRAFTER—A worker who prepares clear, complete, and accurate working plans and detail drawings from rough or detailed sketches or notes for engineering or manufacturing purposes according to specified dimensions—may specialize in architectural, aeronautics, electrical, or other area.

ECOLOGIST—A biological scientist who studies the relationship between organisms and their environments and the effects of pollutants, rainfall, temperature, altitude, and other variables on organisms.

ECONOMIST—A professional who plans, designs, and conducts research to aid in interpretation of economic relationships, and develops solutions for problems arising from the production and distribution of goods and services—may specialize in health, agriculture, labor, or other areas.

EDITOR—A person who prepares materials for publication or release, making revisions or other modifications.

EEG (Electroencephalographic) TECHNOLOGIST—A health care worker who measures impulse frequencies and differences in electrical potential from the brain for use in diagnosis of brain disorders using the electroencephalograph.

EKG (Electrocardiograph) TECHNICIAN—A health care worker who records electromotive variations in the action of heart muscle, using the electrocardiograph machine, to help determine the causes of heart complications.

EMERGENCY MEDICAL TECHNICIAN—A health care worker who administers first aid, including life support, while transporting sick or injured persons to a medical facility.

ENDOCRINOLOGIST—A doctor who specializes in infertility problems (ovulation, hormones, male infertility, diagnostic method, in-vitro fertilization, egg implantation, etc.).

ENGINEER—A professional who applies mathematical and scientific principles in an economical and efficient manner to the design, planning, development, production, supervision, repair, and maintenance of the products, equipment, structures, processes, systems, and programs of industrial societies. The main branches of engineering are civil, electrical/electronics, mechanical, industrial, metallurgical, chemical, aerospace, agricultural, and nuclear.

ENTOMOLOGIST—A professional scientist who studies insects and their relation to plant and animal life, identifies and classifies insects, and helps to develop pesticides and other methods to control pests.

ENTREPRENEUR—An individual who starts and owns his or her own business.

ENVIRONMENTAL ENGINEER—Usually a civil, chemical, or mechanical engineer who specializes in some aspect of the environment (i.e., soil testing, air pollution, water pollution, toxic substances, etc.).

ENVIRONMENTALIST—A professional who studies, analyzes, and evaluates environmental problems and applies scientific knowledge to prevent pollution, solve problems, and make predictions about the air, water, land, noise, and radioactivity.

ENVIRONMENTAL HEALTH TECHNICIAN—A worker who conducts tests and field investigations to obtain information for use by environmental engineering and scientific personnel in determining sources and methods of controlling pollutants in air, water, and soil.

ERGONOMIST—A professional who specializes in designing products and arranging work environments to adapt to the behaviors of human beings and to ensure their health and safety on the job.

ESCROW OFFICER—A professional worker who holds in escrow (safekeeping) funds, legal papers, or other collateral posted by contracting parties to ensure fulfillment of contracts or trust agreements.

ESTIMATOR—An accounting specialist who prepares cost estimates for products or services requested to aid management in bidding on jobs or determining the price of those products or services.

EXECUTIVE HOUSEKEEPER—An administrator who directs an institutional housekeeping program to ensure clean, orderly, and attractive conditions; may be employed by hospitals, hotels, or motels.

FBI AGENT—See Special Agent.

FINANCIAL AID DIRECTOR—A professional who directs the scholarship, grant, and loan programs at a college or university to provide financial assistance to students.

FINANCIAL ANALYST—A worker who conducts statistical analyses of information affecting an investment program of a public, industrial, or financial institution such as a bank, insurance company, brokerage, or investment house.

FINANCIAL PLANNER—A professional who specializes in helping individuals and companies invest their income in the most efficient and economical manner to better prepare for future needs, goals, and emergencies.

FLORICULTURIST—A professional horticulturist who specializes in the research, breeding, production, storage, processing, and transit of flowers.

FOOD AND DRUG INSPECTOR—A government worker who inspects establishments where food, drugs, cosmetics, and similar consumer items are manufactured, handled, stored, or sold to enforce legal standards of sanitary conditions and health and hygiene habits of persons handling such products.

FOOD SCIENTIST—A professional scientist who applies scientific and engineering principles in the research, development, production technology, quality control, packaging, processing, and utilization of foods—may specialize in dairy products, poultry, cereal, grains, etc.

FOOD SERVICE MANAGER—An individual who manages, supervises, and coordinates a program of serving food in a hospital, nursing home, college, or other institution.

FOREIGN SERVICE OFFICER—A government worker who represents the interest of the United States government and citizens by conducting relations with foreign governments and international organizations, protecting and advancing political, economic, and commercial interests, and rendering personal services to Americans abroad and to foreign nationals traveling to the United States—may be termed diplomat, consultant, ambassador, etc.

FORESTER—A professional who manages and protects forest lands and their resources for economic, educational, and recreational purposes.

FORESTRY TECHNICIAN—A worker who gathers information pertaining to size, content, condition, and other characteristics of forest tracts, and under the direction of a forester, leads workers in forest propagation, fire prevention and fighting, and maintenance of facilities.

4-H CLUB AGENT—A worker who organizes and directs the educational projects and activities of a 4-H club; recruits farm volunteer leaders; directs selection of projects such as sewing, woodworking, photography, and livestock raising; and develops and arranges exhibits in county or state fairs.

FREELANCE WRITER—A self-employed writer who submits his or her work to various sources for publication and/or writes on a contract basis.

FUNERAL DIRECTOR—An individual who arranges, coordinates, and directs burial preparations and funeral services.

GENEALOGIST—A historian who conducts research into the background of an individual or family in order to establish descent or to discover and identify forbears of the individual or family.

GENERAL CONTRACTOR—See Contractor.

GENERAL PRACTITIONER—A medical doctor who treats a variety of medical problems without specializing in any one area.

GENERAL SUPERINTENDENT—A manager who directs the activities of workers in the construction of buildings, dams, highways, pipelines, or other structures; usually directs and oversees other supervisory personnel.

GENETICIST—A professional scientist who studies the hereditary variation of characteristics in forms of life—may specialize in molecular, population, human, medical, animal, or plant areas.

GEODESIST—A professional who studies the size, shape, and gravitational field of the earth.

GEOGRAPHER—A professional who studies nature and the features of the earth, relating and interpreting interactions of physical and cultural phenomena.

GEOMORPHOLOGIST—A geologist who specializes in the history, structure, and changes of the earth's surface.

GEOPHYSICIST—A physical scientist who studies the physical aspects of earth, including its atmosphere and hydrosphere. Specialties include oceanography, glaciology, and volcanology.

GEOTECHNICAL ENGINEER—A civil engineer who specializes in the evaluation of soil and rocks that support structures and assists in the design and construction of foundations, dams, tunnels, and other structures.

GERIATRIC CASE MANAGER—A professional social worker who specializes in diagnosing the physical and mental health needs and arranging for the proper care of the elderly.

GERONTOLOGIST—A sociologist who specializes in the study of aging and older adults.

GLAZIER—A construction worker who installs glass in windows, skylights, store fronts, display cases, building fronts, interior walls, ceilings, and table tops—may specialize in auto-glass, aircraft, plate-glass, etc.

GRAPHIC DESIGNER—An artist who designs books, magazines, newspapers, packaging, and other printed materials as well as artwork for TV and other media.

GREENSKEEPER—A worker who oversees a staff in preserving the grounds and turf of golf courses.

GROUNDSKEEPER—A caretaker who maintains the grounds of industrial, commercial, or public property and performs a combination of tasks such as cutting lawns, trimming hedges, pruning trees, fertilizing and spraying, raking and planting, watering, and shoveling snow.

GYNECOLOGIST—A medical doctor who specializes in the diagnosis, treatment, and prevention of diseases and disorders of the female genital, urinary, and rectal organs.

HAND MOLDER—A worker who tends a stuffing machine that fills molds with meat emulsion to form meat loaves—may stuff bologna and sausages into casings by hand.

HEALTH ADVOCATE—A health care professional who serves as a liaison between patients and health care institutions; provides a link to appropriate services.

HEALTH MICROBIOLOGIST—See Microbiologist.

HOME ECONOMIST—A professional who organizes and conducts consumer education service or research programs for equipment, food, textile, or utility companies utilizing principles of home economics (preparing food, recipe testing, using household equipment and products, home management, etc.)—may specialize as a nutritionist, equipment specialist, or in another area.

HOME HEALTH AIDE—A worker who cares for elderly, convalescent (recovering from illness), or disabled persons in the patient's home, performing any combination of tasks such as changing beds, ironing, washing, purchasing food items, giving massages, assisting patient in walking, and monitoring the patient's condition.

HORTICULTURIST—A professional who conducts experiments and investigations in the breeding, production, storage, processing, and transport of fruits, nuts, berries, vegetables, flowers, bushes, and trees.

HOTEL/MOTEL MANAGER—A person who manages a hotel or motel to ensure it is an efficient and profitable operation and is meeting the guests' service needs.

HYDRAULICS ENGINEER—A civil engineer who specializes in the area of hydraulics (operation or motion by means of water or liquid).

HYDROGRAPHER—An individual who analyzes hydrographic data to determine trends in movement and utilization of water.

HYDROLOGIST—A geologist who studies the distribution, circulation, and physical properties of underground and surface waters.

ILLUSTRATOR—A worker who creates drawings or other images for display, book or magazine illustration, or advertising purposes using pencil, pen, charcoal, watercolors, air brush, or computer.

INDUSTRIAL DESIGNER—A professional who conceives and designs the forms of manufactured products.

INDUSTRIAL HYGIENIST—A health care professional who develops, conducts, and evaluates the health program in an industrial setting or governmental organization in an effort to identify, eliminate, and control health hazards such as dust, gases, vapors, lighting, noise, ventilation, and diseases.

INDUSTRIAL TRUCK DRIVER—A worker who drives a gasoline, natural gas, or electric-powered industrial truck equipped with lifting devices (forklifts, boom, scoop, lift beam, swivel hook, fork-grapple, clamps, elevating platform, or trailer hitch) to push, pull, stack, tier, or move products, equipment, or materials in a warehouse, storage yard, or factory.

INFORMATION SCIENTIST—A professional who designs computerized information systems to provide management or clients with specific electronic data utilizing data processing principles, mathematics, and computer capabilities.

INSTRUMENT REPAIRER—A worker who repairs and calibrates speedometers and other automotive gauges and meters using hand tools and test equipment.

INSTRUMENTATION TECHNICIAN—A skilled worker who develops and operates electronic equipment and related apparatus used to test mechanical and/or electrical equipment.

INSURANCE ADJUSTER—A worker who investigates claims against insurance or other companies for personal, casualty, or property loss or damages, and attempts to effect an out-of-court settlement with the claimant—may be called a claims adjuster.

INTERIOR DESIGNER—A professional who plans, designs, and finishes interior environments of residential, commercial, and industrial buildings— may specialize in the decorative aspect and be called an interior decorator.

INTERNAL AUDITOR—See Auditor.

INTERNAL REVENUE AGENT—A government officer who conducts independent field audits and investigations of federal income tax returns to verify or amend tax liabilities.

INTERNIST—A medical doctor who specializes in the diagnosis, treatment, and prevention of diseases, conditions, and injuries of human internal organs and systems.

JOB ANALYST—A professional who collects, analyzes, and prepares information on various occupations; observes jobs and interviews workers; writes job descriptions and specifications—may specialize in classifying positions.

JOB SETTER—A machinist who sets up and adjusts various machine tools such as lathes, milling, and boring machines, drill and punch presses, etc.; usually works by blueprint, job order, and other specifications.

LANDSCAPE ARCHITECT—A professional who plans and designs the development of land areas for parks, airports, highways, parkways, hospitals, schools, factories, housing projects, business establishments, and other projects.

LANDSCAPE GARDENER—A worker who plans and executes small-scale landscaping operations and maintains grounds of businesses and private residences.

LATHER—A construction worker who fastens wooden, metal, or rockboard (lathe) to walls, ceilings, and partitions of buildings to provide supporting base for plaster, fireproofing, or acoustical material, using hand tools and portable power tools (not to be confused with someone who uses a tool called a lathe).

LAYOUT WORKER—A worker who lays out metal stock or work pieces such as castings, plates, or machine parts to indicate location, dimensions, and tolerances necessary for further processing; analyzes specifications and computing dimensions; and follows blueprints.

LEGAL INVESTIGATOR—A legal assistant who researches and prepares cases relating to administrative appeals of civil service members; also presents arguments and evidence to support appeals hearings.

LEGAL SECRETARY—A secretary who prepares legal papers and correspondence of a legal nature such as summonses, complaints, motions, and subpoenas.

LIBRARY TECHNICIAN—One who provides information services, including answering cataloging questions, assisting users with research tools, filing cards, answering routine inquiries, and making referrals.

LICENSED PRACTICAL NURSE—A health care worker, licensed by the state, who provides direct bedside care for those who are sick, injured, or elderly in hospitals, clinics, private homes, convalescent homes, and other institutions.

LINE INSTALLER—A worker who, using electrician's hand tools, installs and repairs telephone and telegraph lines, poles, and related equipment according to diagrams and other specifications.

LINGUIST—A professional who studies the components, structure, nature, and modification of language and speech and may help to prepare language-teaching materials, dictionaries, and handbooks.

LITHOGRAPHIC PLATE MAKER—A worker who transfers positive or negative images to offset printing plates using various methods.

LOBBYIST—A public relations specialist who contacts and meets with members of the legislature and other public officials to persuade them to support laws that are favorable to a client's interest.

MACHINIST—A worker who, applying knowledge of mechanics and machinery procedures, sets up and operates machine tools and fits and assembles parts to make or repair metal parts, mechanisms, tools, or machines.

MAITRE D'HOTEL—The head waiter or steward of a hotel or restaurant.

MANPOWER DIRECTOR—An administrator who directs and supervises employees and activities aimed at securing qualified temporary workers to fill job vacancies.

MANUFACTURERS' SALES REPRESENTATIVE—A salesperson who sells single, allied, diversified, or multiline products to wholesalers or other customers for one or more manufacturers on a commission basis.

MARBLESETTER—A construction worker who cuts, tools, and sets marble slabs in the floors and walls of a building and repairs and polishes existing slabs.

MARKET RESEARCH ANALYST—A professional who researches marketing conditions and trends in a local, regional, or national area to determine the potential sales of a product or service.

MEDICAL ASSISTANT—One who serves as a secretary, receptionist, and/or bookkeeper and performs duties such as arranging for x-ray and other medical procedures, billing and collecting fees, and filing insurance claims.

MEDICAL ENGINEER—An engineer who works with physicians and scientists to apply engineering principles to medical diagnosis, surgery, and rehabilitation.

MEDICAL ILLUSTRATOR—An artist who sketches, draws, paints, and develops diagrams and models illustrating medical findings for use in publications, exhibits, consultations, research, and teaching.

MEDICAL LAB TECHNICIAN—A health care worker who performs routine laboratory tests, such as taking blood samples, for use in the treatment and diagnosis of disease.

MEDICAL OFFICER—A public service worker who plans and participates in medical research programs in hospitals, clinics, or other public medical facilities to provide medical services to those who qualify.

MEDICAL RECORDS TECHNICIAN—An individual who specializes in compiling and maintaining medical records of hospital and clinic patients.

MEDICAL TECHNOLOGIST—A medical specialist who performs chemical, microscopic, serologic, hematologic, immunohematologic, parasitic, and bacteriologic tests to provide information for use in treatment and diagnosis of disease.

MENTAL HEALTH TECHNICIAN—A health care worker who assists, treats, works with, and directly supervises emotionally ill and mentally retarded patients.

MENTAL HEALTH WORKER—Any individual—from a secretary to a counselor or an administrator—who works in a hospital or agency that provides treatment and/or services to individuals who experience mental or emotional difficulties.

MERCHANDISE DISPLAYER—A worker who displays merchandise such as clothes, accessories, and furniture in windows, in showcases, and on sales floors of retail stores to attract the attention of prospective customers.

METALLURGIST—A person who researches the physical characteristics, properties, and processing of metals.

METEOROLOGIST—A physical scientist who analyzes and interprets meteorological data gathered by surface and upper-air stations, satellites, and radar to prepare weather reports and forecasts.

MICROBIOLOGIST—A scientist who studies the growth, structure, development, and general characteristics of bacteria and other microorganisms—may specialize in viruses or in other areas.

MILLWRIGHT—A skilled worker who installs machinery and equipment in industrial plants, according to a layout plan, blueprint, and other drawings, using hoists, lift trucks, hand tools, and power tools.

MINERALOGIST—A physicist who examines, analyzes, and classifies minerals, gems, and precious stones.

MODEL MAKER—A skilled worker who constructs scale models of objects using clay, metal, wood, fiberglass, or other substances, depending on the industry for which the model is being constructed (i.e., automobile, boat, etc.).

MULTIMEDIA SPECIALIST/TECHNICIAN—A worker who skillfully blends audio, video, graphics, and text to communicate information, often working solely on a computer.

MUSIC THERAPIST—A health care specialist who plans, organizes, teaches, and supervises music and related activities for a more integrated and successful rehabilitation of patients.

MYCOLOGIST—A scientist who studies the life processes of edible, poisonous, and parasitic fungi to determine which are useful to medicine, agriculture, and industry.

NATURALIST—A professional who specializes in the study of plants or animals (e.g., zoologist, botanist, etc.).

NEUROLOGIST—A medical doctor who specializes in the diagnosis and treatment of organic diseases and disorders of the nervous system.

NUCLEAR ENGINEER—An engineer who engages in the design, development, monitoring, and operation of nuclear power plants to generate electricity and power navy ships—may also conduct research on nuclear energy and radiation.

NUCLEAR MEDICINE TECHNOLOGIST—A medical specialist who prepares, administers, and measures radioactive isotopes in therapeutic, diagnostic, and tracer studies, utilizing a variety of radioisotope equipment—prepares stock solutions of radioactive materials and calculates doses to be administered by a radiologist.

NURSE ANESTHETIST—A professional health care specialist who administers anesthetics or drugs (via fluid, gas, etc.) to lessen or alleviate pain during surgical, dental, or other medical procedures.

NURSE-MIDWIFE—A nurse who specializes in providing medical care to women under the care of an obstetrician—delivers babies and provides patients with health care during pregnancy as well as for a period of time following childbirth.

NURSE PRACTITIONER—A professional health care specialist who usually works with a physician to provide general medical care and treatment to assigned patients; may work independently.

NUTRITIONIST—A professional who conducts and organizes consumer education service or research programs involving food and nutrition.

OBSTETRICIAN—A medical doctor who specializes in the treatment of women during prenatal, natal, and postnatal periods; concerned with the mother's as well as the infant's health and comfort during pregnancy.

OCCUPATIONAL THERAPIST—A health care specialist who plans, organizes, and conducts a comprehensive rehabilitation program to help mentally, emotionally, or physically disabled persons to return to work and resume daily activities.

OCEANOGRAPHER—A specialist who studies oceans, seas, marine life, and related areas.

OPERATING ENGINEER—A heavy equipment operator of one or more types of power construction equipment such as compressor pumps, hoists, derricks, cranes, shovels, tractors, scrapers, or motor graders to excavate, move, and grade earth; erect and reinforce steel; or pour concrete or other hard surface material.

OPHTHALMOLOGIST—A medical doctor who specializes in the diagnosis, treatment, and prevention of diseases and injuries of the eyes.

OPTICIAN—A specialist who makes or orders and sells eyeglasses and contact lenses according to individual prescriptions.

OPTOMETRIST—One who specializes in eye examinations to determine visual efficiency, performance, diseases, and conditions, and prescribes corrective lenses or procedures.

ORTHODONTIST—A dentist who specializes in the prevention, diagnosis, and correction of abnormalities in the arrangement and growth of teeth.

ORTHOTIST—An individual who, in cooperation with a physician, fits and prepares devices for patients with disabling conditions of the limbs and spine.

OSTEOPATH—A medical doctor who specializes in the diagnosis, treatment, and prevention of diseases and injury through an integrated or holistic approach using drugs, surgery, radiation, physical and/or manipulative therapy—particular focus is on the correction of musculoskeletal disorders.

OTOLARYNGOLOGIST—A medical doctor who specializes in the diagnosis, treatment, and prevention of diseases of the ear, nose, and throat.

OUTPLACEMENT SPECIALIST—A professional who assists workers in transitions, particularly those from executive and management backgrounds who have been laid off or fired, to find other employment; may help with career planning and job hunting techniques and by providing referrals.

PALEONTOLOGIST—A professional who studies the fossilized remains of plants and animals found in geological formations to trace the evolution and development of past life and identify geological formations according to nature and chronology.

PARALEGAL—A law clerk who studies law, researches facts, and prepares documents to assist lawyers.

PARASITOLOGIST—A professional scientist who studies characteristics, habits, and life cycles of animal parasites such as protozoans, tapeworms, roundworms, and flukes to determine the manner in which they attack humans and animals and the effects thereof.

PARK RANGER—An officer who enforces laws, regulations, and policies in state or national parks.

PAROLE/PROBATION OFFICER—A professional social worker involved in the conditional release of juvenile or adult offenders from correctional institutions; establishes relationships, provides supervision, and evaluation, and performs other duties.

PATENT AGENT—A professional worker who prepares and presents patent applications to the U.S. Patent Office and in patent courts.

PATENT LAWYER—A lawyer who specializes in advising clients such as inventors, investors, and manufacturers concerning the patentability of inventions, infringements, validity, and similar items; prosecutes and defends clients.

PATHOLOGIST—A medical doctor who specializes in determining the nature, cause, and development of diseases, structural and functional changes caused by them, cause of death, and effects of treatment.

PEDIATRICIAN—A medical doctor who specializes in the general medical care of children through adolescence.

PEDODONTIST—A professional dental specialist who specializes in the treatment of children's teeth.

PENOLOGIST—A professional sociologist who specializes in research on punishment for crime, crime control and prevention, management of penal institutions (jails and prisons), and rehabilitation.

PERFUSIONIST—A health care worker who operates equipment designed to support or temporarily replace a patient's circulatory or respiratory functions.

PERSONNEL DIRECTOR—An individual who plans and carries out policies relating to all phases of personnel activity—recruits workers, interviews, fills vacancies, plans and conducts new employee orientations, keeps records of promotions, insurance, transfers, and hires—may be called a Human Resources Manager.

PETROLOGIST—A professional who studies the composition, structure, and history of the rock masses that form the earth's crust.

PHARMACIST—A medical professional who specializes in mixing chemical compounds and dispensing medications prescribed by physicians, dentists, and other health care professionals; also makes recommendations regarding over-the-counter drugs.

PHARMACOLOGIST—A biological scientist who specializes in the study of drugs, gases, dusts, and other materials and their effect on the tissue and physiological processes of animals and human beings.

PHOTOENGRAVER—A worker who photographs copy, develops negatives, and prepares photosensitized metal plates such as copper, zinc, aluminum, and magnesium for use in printing, using photography and developing equipment and engraver's tools.

PHOTOGRAMMETRIST—A surveyor who specializes in the preparation of maps and drawings by measuring and interpreting aerial photographs using analytical processes and mathematical formulas.

PHOTO-OPTICS TECHNICIAN—A worker who sets up and operates photo-optical instrumentation to record and photograph data for scientific and engineering projects.

PHYCOLOGIST—A life scientist who specializes in the study of seaweeds or algae.

PHYSIATRIST—A medical doctor who specializes in the clinical and diagnostic use of physical agents and exercise to provide physiotherapy for physical, mental, and occupational well-being.

PHYSICAL THERAPIST—A health care specialist who plans and administers medically prescribed treatment programs to relieve pain and treat malfunctions in the neuromuscular and other systems caused by disease, injury, or loss of body parts.

PHYSIOLOGIST—A professional scientist who conducts research on cellular structure and organ-system functions of plants and animals, studying growth, respiration, circulation, excretions, movement, reproduction, and other functions.

PIPEFITTER—A plumbing specialist who lays out, builds, assembles, installs, and maintains piping and piping systems, fixtures, and equipment for steam, hot water, heating, cooling, lubricating, sprinkling, and industrial processing systems.

PLANT BREEDER —A professional who plans and conducts breeding studies to develop and improve varieties of crops—seeks to improve size, quality, yield, maturity, and resistance to disease, frost, and pests.

PLASTERER—A construction worker who applies coats of plaster to the interior walls, ceilings and partitions of buildings to produce a finished surface.

PLASTIC SURGEON—A medical doctor who specializes in skin graphs and bone tissue replacement, transplants, and restoration and repair of lost, deformed, or injured parts of the face and body.

PLAYWRIGHT—A professional who writes original plays such as tragedies, comedies, or dramas, or adapts themes from fictional, historical, or narrative sources for dramatic presentation.

PODIATRIST—A medical doctor who specializes in the diagnosis, treatment, and prevention of foot diseases, conditions, and deformities.

POLICE COMMISSIONER—A professional government worker who administers a municipal (city) police department.

POLYGRAPH EXAMINER—See Administrative Examiner.

PROCTOLOGIST—A medical doctor who specializes in the diagnosis and treatment of diseases and disorders of the anus, rectum, and colon; performs surgical removal of diseased or malfunctioning parts and prescribes medication or other procedures when necessary.

PRODUCTION SUPERINTENDENT—A manager who, utilizing knowledge of product technology, production methods and procedures, and capabilities of machines and equipment, directs and coordinates other supervisory personnel in activities concerned with the production of a company's products.

PROSTHETIST—A worker who, working with a physician, provides care to patients with partial or total absence of limbs by planning the construction and fitting of devices.

PSYCHIATRIC SOCIAL WORKER—A professional social worker who specializes in providing psychiatric social work assistance to mentally or emotionally disturbed patients at hospitals, clinics, and other medical centers, as well as to their families, collaborating with a psychiatric and allied team in providing a diagnosis and treatment plan.

PSYCHIATRIST—A medical doctor who specializes in the study, diagnosis, and treatment of mental, emotional, and behavioral disorders.

PSYCHOLOGIST—A professional who specializes in the research, collection, interpretation, and application of scientific information about human behavior and mental processes—may specialize in experimental, educational, social, clinical, counseling, school, industrial, engineering, or developmental psychology.

PSYCHOMETRIST—A professional who administers, scores, and interprets intelligence, aptitude, achievement, and other psychological tests.

PUBLIC HEALTH EDUCATOR—An individual who plans, organizes, and directs health education programs for groups and communities; prepares and distributes educational information materials; conducts surveys; and offers workshops.

PUBLIC HEALTH SERVICE OFFICER—A health care professional who administers a public-health program for a county or city; inspects public facilities for health hazards; may help establish free clinics, impose quarantines, or close establishments for safety reasons.

PUBLIC RELATIONS SPECIALIST—A professional worker who specializes in the planning and conducting of a public relations program designed to create and maintain a favorable public image for an employer or client.

PUPPETEER—An entertainer who stages puppet shows, moving controls of puppets to animate them; also may design and construct puppets.

PURCHASING AGENT—A professional worker who purchases raw materials or other unprocessed goods for processing machinery, equipment, tools, parts, produce, or other supplies, or services necessary for the operation of an organization or business.

RADIATION THERAPY TECHNOLOGIST—A health care specialist who assists radiologists in the treatment of disease by exposing the affected areas to prescribed doses of x-ray or other ionizing radiation; maintains operation controls; assists in treatment responsibilities and record-keeping.

RADIOGRAPHER—A health care specialist who applies roentgen rays and radioactive substances to patients for diagnostic and therapeutic purposes—x-ray technicians may do the actual equipment operation and body positioning.

RADIOLOGIST—A medical doctor who specializes in the diagnosis and treatment of disease using x-ray and radioactive substances to examine organs, make diagnoses, and administer treatments.

RECREATIONAL THERAPIST—A health care specialist who plans, organizes, and directs medically approved recreation programs for patients in hospitals and other institutions.

REGISTERED NURSE—A professional health care worker who specializes in providing those who are sick, injured, or elderly with direct personal care, support, and ongoing medical supervision.

REGISTRAR—A professional who directs and coordinates registration activities at a college or university, handling transcripts and credit evaluations, coordinating class schedules, and preparing statistical reports.

RELIGIOUS BROTHER/RELIGIOUS SISTER—In the Catholic Church, a member of a religious community (e.g., Benedictines, Carmelites, etc.) living vows of poverty, chastity, and obedience in the service of God. Religious brothers may or may not be priests.

OPERATIONS RESEARCH ANALYST—A professional who analyzes management and operational problems and develops solutions using mathematics and computer simulation.

RESPIRATORY THERAPIST—A health care worker who administers respiratory therapy and life support to patients with deficiencies and abnormalities of the cardiopulmonary system under the supervision of a physician and by prescription.

RIGGER—A worker who assembles rigging (material used to hold something together) to lift and move equipment or material at a manufacturing plant, shipyard, or a construction site.

SAFETY ENGINEER—An engineer who specializes in the design, development, implementation, and evaluation of safety programs, apparatus, and other equipment to prevent or correct unsafe environmental working conditions utilizing knowledge of industrial processes, mechanics, chemistry, psychology, and industrial health and safety laws.

SANITARY ENGINEER—A public health engineer who designs and directs the construction and operation of hygienic projects such as waterworks, sewage systems, garbage and trash disposal plants, drainage systems, and insect/rodent control projects.

SCHOOL SUPERINTENDENT—An administrator who directs and coordinates the activities and administration of a state, city, or county school system in accordance with board of education standards—the highest ranking administrator in a school system.

SECURITIES ANALYST—See Financial Analyst.

SECURITIES CLERK—A worker who compiles and maintains records of a firm's securities (stock purchases) transactions.

SECURITIES SALES AGENT—One who buys and sells in a trading division of an investment and brokerage firm.

SECURITY OFFICER—A worker who plans and establishes the security procedures for a company engaged in manufacturing products or processing duty or materials for the federal government.

SEISMOLOGIST—A geologist who studies and interprets seismic (earthquake) data to locate earthquakes and earthquake faults.

SHEET METAL WORKER—A worker who fabricates, assembles, installs, and repairs sheet metal products and equipment such as control boxes, drainpipes, ventilators, and furnace casings according to job order or blueprint.

SILVICULTURIST—A professional who establishes and cares for forest stands and manages tree nurseries and other forests to encourage natural growth of sprouts and seedlings of designated variety.

SOCIAL WORKER—A professional worker who provides assistance through counseling, activities, referrals, and other means, to individuals and groups challenged by poverty, illness, family troubles, antisocial behavior, financial mismanagement, inadequate housing, and other concerns—may specialize in medical, psychiatric, industrial, school, child welfare, family, or other areas.

SOCIOLOGIST—A professional who researches the developmental, structural, cultural, and behavioral patterns of human beings and societies—may specialize in criminology, industrial, rural, social problems, gerontology, urban, medical, or other areas.

SOFTWARE SALESPERSON—A worker who sells, either wholesale or retail, computer programs and/or related materials.

SOIL CONSERVATIONIST—A professional who plans and develops coordinated practices for soil erosion control, moisture conservation, and efficient soil use.

SOIL SCIENTIST—A scientist who studies soil characteristics, maps soil types, and monitors results of soil management techniques.

SOUS CHEF—A chef who supervises and coordinates the activities of cooks and other workers in preparing and cooking foodstuffs.

SPECIAL AGENT—An investigator of alleged or suspected criminal violations of federal, state, or local laws who determines if evidence is sufficient to recommend prosecution; obtains evidence, maintains surveillance, performs undercover work, makes reports, testifies, etc.

SPECIAL EDUCATION TEACHER—A teacher who specializes in the education of the mentally retarded, emotionally troubled, or physically disabled.

SPEECH PATHOLOGIST—A professional who specializes in the diagnosis, treatment, and prevention of speech and language problems; may also research human communications.

SPORTS MARKETER—A public relations and advertising specialist who works to increase and/or maintain spectator patronization of a particular sporting endeavor.

STATISTICIAN—A professional mathematician who plans information collection; analyzes and interprets numerical information from experiments, studies, surveys, and other sources; and applies statistical methodology to provide for further research or statistical analysis.

STOCKBROKER—A professional who buys and sells stocks and bonds for individuals and organizations as a representative of a stock brokerage firm applying knowledge of securities, market conditions, government regulations, and financial circumstances of customers.

STONE MASON—A construction worker who sets stone to build stone structures such as piers, walls, and abutments, or lays walks, curbstones, or other special types of masonry using mason's tools.

STRATIGRAPHER—A professional who studies the relative position and order of succession of deposits containing or separating archeological fossil or plant material.

STRUCTURAL ENGINEER—An engineer who directs or participates in developing, designing, and reviewing building plans to determine load, size, shape, strength, and material requirements necessary for structural integrity.

SURGICAL TECHNICIAN—A health care worker who performs such tasks as washing, shaving, and sterilizing before, during, and after surgical operations.

SURVEYOR—A worker who specializes in the inspection of the earth's surface by measuring angles and distances to determine location, elevation, lines, areas, and contours for purposes of construction, mapmaking, land divisions, title claims, mining, etc.

SYSTEMS ANALYST—A professional who analyzes business or operating procedures to devise the most efficient methods of accomplishing work.

SYSTEMS PROGRAMMER—A professional who develops and writes computer programs to store, locate, and retrieve documents, data, and information for science, engineering, medicine, language, law, military, library science, and other purposes.

TAILOR—A worker who applies principles of garment design, construction, and styling to the construction of new clothing or, more commonly, to the alteration of ready-made apparel.

TAXONOMIST—A plant or animal scientist who specializes in the identification and classification of species and organisms.

TECHNICAL ILLUSTRATOR—A drafter who lays out and draws illustrations for reproduction in reference works, instructions, brochures, and technical manuals showing the assembly, installation, operation, maintenance, and repair of machines, tools, and equipment.

TECHNICAL WRITER—An individual who develops, writes, and edits materials for reports, manuals, briefs, proposals, instruction books, catalogs, and other technical and administrative publications.

TECHNICIAN—A worker who, in direct support of engineers or scientists, uses theoretical knowledge of scientific, engineering, mathematical, or draft design principles to solve practical problems.

TERRAZZO WORKER—A construction worker who applies cement, sand, pigment (color), and marble chips to floors, stairways, and cabinet fixtures to create durable and decorative surfacing according to specifications and drawings.

TISSUE TECHNOLOGIST—A medical specialist who cuts, stains, mounts, and prepares tissue for examination by a pathologist; may assist in autopsies.

TITLE ATTORNEY—A lawyer who specializes in examining abstracts of titles, leases, contracts, and other legal documents to determine ownership of land, gas, oil, and mineral rights; may assist in related trials.

TOOL-AND-DIE MAKER—A skilled worker who analyzes specifications, lays out metal stock, sets up and operates machine tools, and fits and assembles parts to make and repair metal-working dies, cutting tools, jigs, fixtures, gauges, and machinist hand tools.

TOOL PROGRAMMER—A skilled worker who plans a numerical control tape program to control contour-path machining of metal parts on automatic machine tools by means of magnetic or perforated tape.

TOXICOLOGIST—A professional who studies the nature and effects of toxins (poisons) and the treatment of poisoning.

TRAFFIC MANAGER—An individual who directs and coordinates the activities of an organization, including the routing and transportation of goods and products, scheduling, and loading.

TREE SURGEON—A worker who prunes and treats ornamental and shade trees in yards and parks to improve their appearance, health, and value.

TRUST ADMINISTRATOR—A professional who directs and coordinates the creation and administration of private, corporate, probate, and guardianship trusts (safeguarding of goods or items) in accordance with a trust, will, or court order.

TUTOR—A teacher of academic subjects such as English, mathematics, and foreign language to pupils requiring private instruction, adapting the curriculum to meet their needs.

TYPESETTER—A worker who arranges type—by computer or by hand—in preparation for printing.

UNDERWRITER—A worker who reviews individual insurance applications to evaluate the degree of risk involved and either declines or accepts them.

UPHOLSTERER—A skilled worker who engages in spreading, marking, cutting, and sewing fabric padding, covering, and trimming to articles such as furniture, mattresses, and vehicle seats—may work on new furniture or the renovation of older items.

URBAN PLANNER—A professional who develops comprehensive plans and programs for the utilization of land and physical facilities of cities, counties, and metropolitan areas.

UROLOGIST—A medical doctor who specializes in the diagnosis, treatment, and prevention of genitourinary diseases and disorders.

VIROLOGIST—A microbiologist who specializes in the study of viruses and the diseases they cause.

VOCATIONAL REHABILITATION COUNSELOR—A professional counselor who specializes in counseling disabled individuals in job readiness, placement, preparation, and training.

WEBMASTER—A computer specialist who is responsible for overseeing all aspects of a company's or organization's Web site (includes design, development, operations, performance, and maintenance).

WELDER—A worker who is skilled in joining, surfacing, building, or repairing structures or parts of weldable materials using such processes as arc, gas, resistance, solid state, and others.

WHOLESALER—One who manages a store that sells a specific line of merchandise such as groceries, meat, liquor, apparel, jewelry, appliances, furniture, or other items to retailers, who then sell directly to consumers.

WIRELESS SPECIALIST—A technician who specializes in the design and service of small high-tech instruments such as cellular phones, fax machines, and pagers.

Appendix B
Definitions of Selected Skill Statements

ABSTRACT REASONING—The ability to work with and apply ideas and concepts that are difficult to understand; also, the ability to think through that which is not concrete or easily understood from a practical perspective.

AGILITY—Quality of nimbleness or being quick and light-footed; performing body movements with ease.

ANALYZE—The ability to effectively look at an item, event, or situation to determine its nature and how to gain a better understanding.

ANALYZE OR LISTEN INTROSPECTIVELY—The ability to understand the various aspects of one's own or another's behavior; the ability to interpret feelings, thoughts, and behaviors effectively.

APPROPRIATE DECISIONS—The ability to make effective decisions at the right time, usually resulting in a suitable outcome.

APTITUDE FOR ACCURACY AND DETAIL—The ability to carefully perform tasks that involve much detail.

CHARISMA—The ability to draw or attract others to listen, observe, or follow.

FINGER DEXTERITY—The ability to move one's fingers rapidly or accurately when handling small items or objects.

FORMULATE AND DEFEND POSITION—The ability to present and back up with factual evidence or a belief, opinion, or position.

FORM PERCEPTION—The ability to notice details in objects, pictures, or other materials and to see fine differences in shape, shading, figures, and widths and lengths of lines.

INTERPERSONAL COMMUNICATION—The ability to skillfully give, listen to, and understand messages to and from other people through the use of words, listening techniques, eye contact, body language, actions, etc.

INTERPRET—The ability to provide a definition for something in a manner that can be more clearly understood by others.

KEEN OBSERVATION—Alertness; the ability to pick up detail and notice things others may miss.

LOGICAL THINKING—Thinking in which opinions and decisions are based on factual evidence; the ability to arrive at a decision following standard and predictable reasoning procedures.

MAINTAIN COMPOSURE IN STRESSFUL SITUATIONS OR UNDER PRESSURE—The ability to remain rational and calm in the face of danger, frustration, fear, disaster, or unexpected events.

MAKE ANALOGIES—The ability to make connections, often relating similar events, situations, and problems that occured under different circumstances.

MANUAL DEXTERITY—The ability to work skillfully with one's hands, accomplishing tasks deftly and accurately.

MOTOR COORDINATION—The ability to work one's fingers or hands in coordination with one's eyes to accomplish tasks accurately and with speed.

OBJECTIVITY—The ability to listen or react to a statement, event, or situation in a factual manner without allowing negative or positive impressions to interfere with one's reaction; the tendency to keep responses relatively free from biased emotions and feelings.

PHYSICAL STAMINA—Having the physical strength to endure periods of sickness, disease, fatigue, etc.

READ OR SPEAK ARTICULATELY—The ability to read aloud or speak clearly using correct pronunciation.

SOLVE QUANTITATIVE PROBLEMS—The ability to figure out answers to problems that involve numbers, measurement, or mathematics.

SOUND JUDGMENT—The ability to look at an event, situation, or problem from all angles, using decision-making techniques along with one's education, training, and experiences to determine what is occurring and how to react to it.

SPATIAL PERCEPTION—The ability to look at blueprints, flat drawings, or diagrams and accurately visualize how the structure will appear in physical form, including height, width, and depth.

SYNTHESIZE INFORMATION—The ability to integrate or put together parts to arrive at a solution or answer or to create a whole.

Appendix C
Definitions of Values and Personal Attributes

ACHIEVEMENT—Making progress; successfully completing or accomplishing a goal or task.

ADAPTABILITY—The ability to adjust to and fit into different situations; the ability to alter one's behavior or thinking in order to suit circumstances.

AESTHETIC AWARENESS—The ability to grasp and appreciate the beauty of an event, performance, situation, or physical or social environment; the ability to relate to the beauty in music, song, dance, pictures, structures, nature, and behavior.

ALERTNESS—The ability to quickly recognize details and things that others may miss; tendency to observe closely and remain watchful.

ANALYTICAL AND LOGICAL THINKING—The ability to look at and understand the various aspects of an event, situation, or item and arrive at a decision, using standard and predictable reasoning procedures.

COMPETITIVE DRIVE—The spirit of challenging and contesting others in order to win or gain something desired; a liking for rivalry and competition with others.

CONSCIENTIOUS—The awareness of what one does and sensitive to how one's behavior may be affecting another; honorable and responsible.

CURIOSITY AND ENTHUSIASM FOR GADGETRY—The tendency to handle, take apart, ask questions, and be excited about manipulating items and objects (machines, etc.).

DECISIVENESS—The ability to decide without delay; making a decision to act firmly and without doubt.

DEDICATION—Being so strongly committed to something that you are willing to go through much discomfort, if necessary, to achieve the end result; being loyal; giving one's total effort.

DEPENDABILITY—Being trustworthy, reliable, and responsible; can be counted on to come through and to behave as expected.

DILIGENCE—The quality of working steadily at a task until done.

DIPLOMATIC—Being careful to do what is appropriate and to consider the various sides of an issue; ability to manage and negotiate with others without hurting their feelings.

DISCREET—Showing good judgment; not likely to do something without thoughtful consideration; capable of keeping quiet about a private or controversial matter.

EMPATHY—The ability to genuinely relate to other people by imagining their emotions and feelings; the ability to put yourself in another person's shoes, as it were.

ENDURANCE—The ability to withstand discomfort, painful circumstances, hardship, boredom, or stress.

FRAME INQUIRY AND RESPOND OBJECTIVELY—Ability to ask questions that can be logically and scientifically researched as well as respond to others relatively free from biased emotions and feelings.

IMAGINATION—The ability to think and form images of things, events, or ideas which do not presently exist or have never existed.

INDEPENDENCE—The desire to think or perform tasks and activities without being helped, controlled, or assisted; liking to do things on one's own; freedom from authority and confining rules.

INDUSTRIOUS—The ability to work hard, continuously, steadily; diligent; to keep busy.

INITIATIVE—The ability to take the lead; to move ahead or take the first step.

INQUISITIVENESS—Curiosity, wanting answers; desire to gain knowledge.

INTEGRITY—Honesty, truthfulness, and desire to do what is morally right; uprightness; can be trusted to follow through without corruption.

INTELLECTUAL GROWTH—The ability and desire to continually gain knowledge, understanding, and wisdom without stagnation or hindrance.

LINGUISTIC ABILITY—The ability to analyze and understand the structure of languages, make comparisons, etc.

LOYALTY—A strong sense of commitment or unbroken support; faithfulness.

MENTAL AND EMOTIONAL WELL-BEING—The ability to remain calm, make appropriate decisions, and control one's emotions in stressful or extremely difficult circumstances; not easily shaken—emotionally or mentally.

PERSEVERANCE—The quality of not quitting; never giving up; steadfastness; to persist in spite of difficulties.

PERSUASIVE—The ability to influence and draw others to think or behave in a certain way.

POISE AND COMPOSURE UNDER CLOSE PUBLIC SCRUTINY AND CRITICISM—The ability to maintain control over one's thoughts and actions and calmly continue in one's tasks or activities while being observed (or having something you are responsible for observed) and/or criticized by others.

PRACTICAL—The tendency to take effective action instead of theorizing or speculating; pragmatic.

REFLECTIVE NATURE—Thoughtful; making mental connections between disparate situations.

RESOURCEFULNESS—The ability to solve problems and get through difficult situations, particularly when standard resources are scarce or nonexistent.

RESPONSIBILITY—Trustworthy and dependable; the ability to adequately carry through, oversee, or supervise; can be relied on to perform as expected.

SECURITY—Safe from danger, hurt, discomfort, or instability; firmly fixed and sure; occupationally, being sure of financial income and job stability.

SELF-DISCIPLINE—The ability to control and positively direct one's emotions, feelings, thoughts, and behavior.

SENSITIVITY TO MULTIPLE PERSPECTIVES—Open and understanding in terms of different viewpoints, techniques, methods of operation, uses, etc.

SENSITIVITY TO THE INCONSISTENCIES OF HUMAN BEHAVIOR—Understanding, helpful, and patient with those who demonstrate abnormal, antisocial, and/or self-defeating behaviors.

SPIRIT OF SCIENTIFIC INQUIRY—Thinking and questioning in a manner and spirit that reflect a preference for and use of scientific laws and procedures.

TACTFULNESS—The ability to say and do the appropriate things at the appropriate times; be sensitive to the feelings of others.

THOROUGHNESS—The tendency to bring an endeavor to completion with attention to detail; leaving nothing undone.

VERSATILITY—The ability to readily change or move into something different; can easily adapt to many circumstances or environments.

WISDOM—Good judgment; the ability to make appropriate decisions; applying knowledge to do what is right and true.

Index of Occupations

Accountant (See various specialties)

Accounting Clerk, 179, 215

Acoustical Engineer, 35, 77

Acoustical Physicist, 35

Actor, 59, 83, 89, 155, 157

Actuary, 11, 38, 71, 134, 215

Administrative Assistant, 8, 179

Administrative Examiner, 125, 215, 236

Administrative Officer, 149

Adult and Vocational Education Teacher, 74, 215

Advertising Executive, 47

Advertising Manager, 38, 131, 170

Advertising Salesperson, 131

Aerodynamist, 14, 161, 216

Aeronautical Engineer, 14, 77, 161, 216

Aerospace Engineer, 14, 35, 134, 137, 161, 216

Aerospace Engineering Technician, 35

Agricultural Engineer, 17, 50

Airplane Pilot, 14, 149, 161, 188

Allergist, 143

Anesthesiologist, 53, 143, 164

Animal Laboratory Technician, 191

Architectural Engineer, 56

Assistant Buyer, 131

Astronomer, 14, 35-36, 98, 134, 161, 163

Astrophysicist, 14, 35, 161, 216

Automotive Engineer, 116, 137

Bacteriologist, 44, 216

Bailiff, 125, 216

Baker, 68, 203

Bank Economist, 38

Bank Officer, 11, 71, 134

Bank Teller, 38, 179

Banquet Manager, 86

Bar Examiner, 122, 216

Bellhop, 114

Bibliographer, 26, 83, 128, 216

Bicycle Repairer, 140

Bilingual Educator, 89

Biochemist, 17, 41, 44, 50, 53, 110, 164, 191, 217, 219

Biologist, 17, 41, 191

Biomedical Engineer, 23, 77, 137, 217

Biomedical Technician, 80

Biophysicist, 35, 161, 164, 217

Biostatistician, 23, 217

Blacksmith, 119, 217·

Blood Bank Specialist, 23

Boilermaker, 119, 203, 217

Book Conservator, 128

Book Store Manager, 83

Bookbinder, 217

Bookkeeper, 11, 134, 230

Border Patrol Officer, 125

Bricklayer, 65, 203

Broadcast Technician, 59, 80

Broiler Cook, 68

Budget Accountant, 11, 38

Building Contractor, 29, 220

Building Engineer, 113

Building Manager, 65, 113

Bus Driver, 188

Butcher, 68, 119, 203

Buyer, 71, 107, 122, 131, 217

Cabinetmaker, 119, 203

Cable Splicer, 140, 217

Cafeteria Manager, 86, 113

Camp Counselor, 171, 174, 186

Camp Director, 173, 176

Campaign Worker, 167

Campus Minister, 176

Campus Religious Coordinator, 176

Cardiologist, 143, 164, 217

Career Counselor, 149, 196-198, 200, 208-210, 214

Carpenter, 65, 203-204

Carpet Installer, 65

Cartographer, 29, 35, 95, 98, 134, 149, 218

Cartographic Technician, 95

Cartoonist, 32

Case Worker, 107, 125, 182, 185

Cashier, 72, 87, 179

Cataloger, 128, 218

Caterer, 68, 218

Cattle Farmer, 17

Ceramic Engineer, 50, 53, 146, 218

Chamber of Commerce President, 47

Chaplain, 176, 218

Chauffeur, 188

Chef, 68, 86, 107, 239

Chemical Engineer, 50, 52-53, 55, 146

Chemical Lab Technician, 17

Chemical Research Engineer, 50

Chemist, 23, 50, 53, 98, 164, 219

Chief Executive Officer, 47, 218

Chief Information Officer, 62

Child Care Worker, 107

Child Welfare Case Worker, 107

Children's Librarian, 128

Chiropractor, 143, 218

Choreographer, 155, 219

Christian Education Worker, 74

Church Camp Director, 176

Church Recreation Director, 173

Cinematographer, 32, 219

Circuit Engineer, 77

Circulation Manager, 219

Circus Performer, 155, 173

City Manager, 47, 167, 185, 219

Civil Engineer, 29, 56, 146, 161, 219, 226-227

Civil Engineering Technician, 29

Civil Engineers, 58

Civil Service Worker, 89

Classifier, 128

Climatologist, 95, 219

Clothing Designer, 107

Club Manager, 113

Coach, 173-174

College Administrator, 158, 219

College Dean, 47, 74

College Professor, 74

College Recreation Instructor, 173

Columnist, 59, 83, 219

Commentator, 59

Commercial Artist, 29, 219

Commercial/Industrial Electronic Equipment Repairer, 140

Communications Engineer, 77

Community Center Director, 173

Community Service Agency Director, 182, 219

Composer, 155

Compositor, 119, 219

Computer-Aided Designer, 62

Computer Applications Engineer, 62

Computer Graphics Technician, 29

Computer Operator, 62

Computer Programmer, 14, 35, 38, 62, 134, 149, 161

Computer Science Engineer, 14, 50, 62, 77, 137

Computer Service Technician, 62, 140

Concert Promoter, 173

Concrete Mason, 65

Conservationist, 17, 44, 92, 95, 110, 191, 220, 239

Construction Engineer, 56, 65, 146

Consultant, 11, 47, 62, 74, 83, 102, 128, 167, 185, 220, 225

Consulting Engineer, 14, 50, 56, 77, 116, 137, 146

Consumer Protection Specialist, 53

Control Engineer, 77, 116

Controller, 11, 71, 131, 149, 188, 220

Convention Manager, 47

Cook, 68, 107, 239

Cooperative Extension Worker, 44, 107, 182, 220

Coordinator of Rehabilitation Services, 102

Copyeditor, 83

Copywriter, 32, 59, 220

Coroner, 220

Corporation Lawyer, 122

Corrections Officer, 125, 220

Correspondent Banking Officer, 38

Cosmetologist, 203-204

Cost Accountant, 11, 38, 71

Costumer, 155

Court Reporter, 179, 220

Credit Analyst, 38

Credit Manager, 11, 38, 134, 220

Criminal Lawyer, 122

Criminologist, 185, 221

Curator, 26, 32, 44, 104, 191, 221

Curriculum Supervisor, 221

Customs Inspector, 89, 221

Cytologist, 44, 221

Cytotechnologist, 20, 221

Dairy Farmer, 17

Dance Instructor, 155, 173

Dance Therapist, 173, 221

Dancer, 155

Data Processing Department Manager, 62

Database Analyst, 62

Database Manager, 62, 221

Day Care Director, 107

Deep Submergence Vehicle Operator, 188

Demographer, 185

Dental Assistant, 20, 22, 179

Dental Hygienist, 20, 23, 221

Dental Lab Technician, 20, 221

Dentist, 20, 23, 143, 221, 233-34

Department Manager, 62, 107

Department Store Manager, 47

Deputy Sheriff, 125

Dermatologist, 143, 221

Design/Building Specialist, 29, 221

Designer, 29, 32, 62, 107, 131, 149, 155, 226-228

Desk Clerk, 114

Detective, 125

Diagnostic Medical Sonographer, 20, 222

Diesel Mechanic, 140

Dietetic Technician, 20, 222

Dietitian, 44, 53, 68, 86, 102, 107, 110, 164, 222

Dining Room Attendant, 86

Diplomat, 89, 158, 167, 222, 225

Direct Salesperson, 131

Director of Admissions, 74, 222

Director of Career Placement, 47, 74, 222

Director of Food Service, 107

Director of Guidance, 74, 222

Director of Marketing, 131

Director of Sales, 113

Director of Student Affairs, 74

Director of Volunteer Services, 102

Disc Jockey, 59, 83

Dispatcher, 188, 222

District Attorney, 122, 125, 220, 222

District Court Judge, 122

Diver, 149

Drafter, 29, 137, 204, 218, 222, 240

Drama Coach, 155

Dressmaker, 107

Driving Instructor, 188

Drug Enforcement Officer, 125

Drug Rehabilitation Counselor, 182

Drywall Applicator, 65

Ecologist, 41, 44, 56, 92, 95, 191, 223

Economist, 11, 38, 71, 73, 86, 95, 104, 107, 131, 182, 223, 227

Editor, 32, 59-60, 83, 89, 158, 223

Education Consultant, 74

Educational Secretary, 179

Educator, 7, 11, 17, 23, 26, 29, 32, 35, 38, 41, 44, 53, 59, 62, 71, 76, 83, 89, 92, 95, 102, 104, 110, 116, 134, 149, 155, 161, 167, 170, 179, 182, 185, 188, 191, 221, 237

EEG Technologist, 20, 223

EKG Technician, 20, 223

Electrical Appliance Repairer, 80

Electrical Engineer, 14, 50, 77, 116, 137, 146, 161

Electrical Engineering Technician, 77, 80

Electrical Technician, 80

Electrician, 65, 77, 204, 229

Electronic Data Processing Auditor, 62

Electronic Equipment Salesperson, 80

Electronic Home Equipment Repairer, 140

Electronic Technician, 149

Electronics Engineer, 35

Electronics Instructor, 77, 80

Elementary School Teacher, 74

Emergency Medical Services Coordinator, 102

Emergency Medical Technician, 20, 164, 203, 223

Employee Assistance Administrator, 170

Employment Counselor, 170

Endocrinologist, 143, 223

Engine Specialist, 140

Engineer (See various specialties)

Engineering Mechanic, 137

Engineering Officer, 149

Engineers, 16, 52, 55, 58, 64, 79, 118, 139, 190, 207, 241

Entomologist, 17, 110, 223

Entrepreneur, 223

Environmental Engineer, 14, 50, 56, 77, 116, 146, 161, 223

Environmental Health Technician, 20, 224

Environmental Scientist, 95, 98

Environmentalist, 224

Escrow Officer, 122, 224

Estimator, 65, 224

Ethnologist, 26

Evangelist, 176

Executive Housekeeper, 86, 102, 107, 113, 224

Executive Secretary, 179

Family Services Social Worker, 182

Farm Equipment Mechanic, 17, 140

Farm Manager, 44, 92

Farmer, 17-18, 44, 192, 220

Fashion Designer, 107

Fashion Illustrator, 32

Fashion Model, 131, 155

FBI/CIA Agent, 89, 104, 167

Field Representative, 131

Field Service Engineer, 77

File Clerk, 179

Film Director, 155

Film Editor, 32, 89, 158

Film Producer, 32

Financial Aid Officer, 38

Financial Planner, 11, 38, 71, 134, 224

Fire Protection Engineer, 50, 77, 116

Firefighter, 125, 203

Fish and Game Warden, 125

Fish Farmer, 17

Fishery Biologist, 191

Fitness Instructor/Specialist, 173

Flight Attendant, 89

Floriculturist, 224

Florist, 17, 32, 41, 44, 110

Food and Beverage Director, 86

Food and Drug Inspector, 107, 224

Food Production Manager, 86, 113

Food Scientist, 17, 41, 44, 50, 53, 68, 107, 110, 225

Food Service Supervisor, 68

Foreign Correspondent, 59, 158

Foreign Service Officer, 71, 89, 104, 167, 222, 225

Foreign Service Secretary, 179

Foreign Service Worker, 185

Forester, 41, 44, 92-94, 110, 191, 225

Forestry Technician, 92, 225

Freelance Artist, 32

Freelance Writer, 83, 104, 158, 212, 225

Front Office Manager, 113

Funeral Director, 41, 164, 225

Game Official, 173

Gastroenterologist, 143

Genealogist, 26, 104, 225

General Contractor, 65, 225

General Duty Nurse, 152

General Maintenance Mechanic, 140

General Manager, 113

General Practitioner, 225

General Superintendent, 65, 225

Geneticist, 41, 44, 53, 92, 110, 164, 226

Geodesist, 98, 226

Geographer, 26, 95, 97-98, 167, 226

Geological Engineer, 50, 56, 146

Geologist, 35, 53, 56, 95, 98, 146, 226-227, 238

Geomorphologist, 95, 226

Geophysical Engineer, 146

Geophysicist, 35, 95, 98, 146, 161, 226

Geotechnical Engineer, 56, 226

Geriatric Case Manager, 226

Geriatrician, 143

Gerontologist, 104, 182, 185, 226

Glazier, 65, 203, 226

Government Worker, 215, 221, 224-225, 236

Graphic Designer, 29, 32, 149, 226

Greenskeeper, 226

Guard, 125-126, 150-151, 216

Guidance Counselor, 170

Gunsmith, 119, 140

Gynecologist, 143, 164, 226

Hand Molder, 119, 227

Hardware Salesperson, 62

Hardware Service Person, 62

Head Nurse, 152

Health Advocate, 227

Health Care Worker, 217, 221, 223, 229-231, 234, 237-238, 240

Health Consultant, 102

Health Educator, 23, 102, 237

Health Information Specialist, 102

Health Microbiologist, 23, 227

Health Services Administrator, 102

Highway Engineer, 56

Historian, 26, 89, 95, 104, 106, 158, 185, 225

Home Economist, 71, 86, 107, 182, 227

Horticulture Therapist, 110

Horticulturist, 17, 41, 44, 110, 224, 227

Hospital Administrator, 23

Hospital Comptroller, 102

Hospital Food Service Manager, 102

Hospital Personnel Director, 102

Hospital Records Administrator, 102

Host/Hostess, 86

Hotel Information Clerk, 89

Hotel/Motel Manager, 47, 86, 107, 227

Human Services Worker, 182, 185

Humane Society Worker, 191

Hydraulics Engineer, 56, 227

Hydrographer, 98, 227

Hydrologist, 56, 98, 227

Illuminating Engineer, 77

Illustrator, 23, 29, 32, 41, 227, 230, 240

Illustrators, 34

Immunologist, 143

Import/Export Clerk, 89

Industrial Electronics Maintenance Worker, 80

Industrial Engineer, 56, 116, 137

Industrial Engineers, 118

Industrial Health Engineer, 53

Industrial Hygienist, 227

Industrial Machine Repairer, 140

Industrial Psychologist, 170

Industrial Truck Operator, 188

Information Scientist, 128, 228

Instrument Maker, 119

Instrument Repairer, 140, 228

Instrumentation Technician, 80, 140, 228

Insulation Worker, 65

Insurance Agent, 11, 38, 71, 131

Insurance Attorney, 122

Intelligence Specialist, 149

Interior Decorator, 32, 107, 228

Interior Designer, 29, 228

Internal Auditor, 11, 38, 228

Internal Revenue Agent, 11, 71, 228

International Accountant, 11

International Banking Officer, 38

International Economist, 95

Internist, 53, 143, 164, 228

Interpreter/Translator, 83, 89, 149

Investment Banker, 11, 38

Ironworker, 65

Jeweler, 32, 119

Job Analyst, 170, 228

Job Superintendent, 65

Journalist, 59, 83, 89, 149, 158

Judge, 122, 158, 167, 222

Kennel Operator, 191

Kitchen Manager, 68

Labor Relations Specialist, 71, 167, 185

Laboratory Analyst, 53

Laboratory Assistant, 17

Laboratory Technician, 98, 149, 161, 218

Landscape Gardener, 17, 44, 110, 229

Lather, 229

Lawyer, 104, 122, 124, 158, 167, 215, 222, 233-34, 241

Layout Worker, 119, 229

Lecturer, 59, 158

Legal Assistant, 229

Legal Investigator, 229

Legal Secretary, 179, 203, 229

Librarian, 41, 62, 74, 83, 104, 128, 130, 158, 215, 218

Library Consultant, 128

Library Director, 128

Library Technical Assistant, 83

Licensed Practical Nurse, 152, 229

Lifeguard, 125, 173

Line Installer, 140, 229

Linguist, 83, 89, 229

Linguistic Anthropologist, 26

Lithographer, 119

Loan Officer, 38

Lobbyist, 59, 83, 167, 230

Locksmith, 119, 140

Locomotive Engineer, 188, 190

Machine Operator, 119

Machine Repairer, 119, 140

Machine Tool Operator, 119

Machinist, 119, 203-204, 228, 230, 241

Magician, 155

Maitre d' Hotel, 86, 89

Management Accountant, 11

Management Consultant, 11

Managing Director, 113

Manufacturers' Sales Representative, 230

Manufacturing Engineer, 116

Marblesetter, 65, 230

Marine Biologist, 191

Marine Electronics Specialist, 80

Marine Engineer, 14

Market Research Analyst, 11, 71, 95, 104, 131, 134, 158, 170, 230

Market Researcher, 107

Marketing Manager, 113

Marriage Counselor, 182

Materials Handling Engineer, 50, 116, 137, 146

Mathematician, 35, 134, 161, 207, 240

Mayor, 167

Mechanical Drafter, 137

Mechanical Engineer, 14, 56, 77, 116, 137, 139, 223

Mechanical Engineering Technician, 137

Media Center Manager, 128

Media Specialist, 59, 83

Medical Assistant, 20, 164, 179, 230

Medical Engineer, 23, 102, 230

Medical Illustrator, 23, 41, 230

Medical Lab Technician, 20, 41, 230

Medical Librarian, 41, 128

Medical Records Administrator, 102

Medical Records Technician, 20, 230

Mental Health Technician, 20, 231

Mental Health Worker, 170, 231

Merchandise Displayer, 107, 155, 231

Merchandise Manager, 131

Merchandising Supervisor, 86

Merchant Mariner, 188

Metallurgical Engineer, 14, 35, 50, 98, 146, 161

Metallurgical Engineering Technician, 146

Metallurgist, 50, 53, 98, 146, 161, 231

Meteorological Technician, 98

Meteorologist, 35, 95, 161, 219, 231

Microbiologist, 17, 23, 41, 164, 191, 216, 227, 231, 242

Military Officer, 125, 167

Millwright, 119, 137, 140, 203-204, 231

Mineralogist, 35, 98, 231

Mining Engineer, 56, 98, 146

Minister, 170, 176, 182, 185

Minister of Music, 176

Missionary, 89, 176

Model Maker, 29, 32, 231

Motion Picture Photographer, 32, 155

Motorboat Operator, 188

Motorcycle Mechanic, 140

Municipal Recreation Director, 173

Museum/Zoo Worker, 191

Music Director, 59, 155

Music Therapist, 152, 173, 231

Musician, 149, 155

Naturalist, 92, 232

Nature Photographer, 191

Neurologist, 143, 232

News Photographer, 8, 59

News Reporter, 167

Nuclear Engineer, 14, 50, 77, 98, 146, 161, 232

Nuclear Medical Technologist, 23, 161

Nuclear Scientist, 53, 134

Nuclear Technician, 161

Nurse (See various specialties)

Nursery Manager, 17, 44, 92

Nurses, 154

Nursing Home Director, 102

Nutritionist, 23, 41, 44, 53, 68, 86, 107, 110, 164, 227, 232

Obstetrician, 143, 232

Occupational Safety and Health Inspector, 102

Occupational Therapist, 41, 152, 170, 232

Occupational Therapy Assistant, 20

Oceanographer, 35, 95, 98, 232

Office Clerk, 179

Office Machine Servicer, 140

Office Manager, 113, 179

Oil Pumper, 188

Operating Engineer, 65, 188, 233

Operating Room Technician, 20

Operations Engineer, 116

Operations Manager, 62

Ophthalmologist, 143, 233

Optical Physicist, 35

Optical Technician, 161

Optician, 20, 233

Optometric Assistant, 20

Optometrist, 143, 233

Orchestra Conductor, 155

Orthodontist, 143, 233

Osteopath, 143, 164, 233

Otolaryngologist, 233

Outplacement Specialist, 170, 233

Package Designer, 131

Painter, 32, 65, 203-204

Paleontologist, 26, 98, 233

Paperhanger, 65

Paralegal, 125, 179, 233

Paramedic, 41

Parasitologist, 17, 41, 233

Park Aide, 93

Park Police, 92

Park Ranger, 92, 110, 173, 191, 234

Parole/Probation Officer, 122, 125, 167, 234

Pastor, 176

Pastry Chef, 68

Patent Agent, 122, 234

Patent Examiner, 53

Patent Lawyer, 122, 234

Pathologist, 89, 143, 164, 170, 191, 221, 234, 239, 241

Peace Corps Worker, 104

Pediatrician, 143, 164, 234

Penologist, 125, 167, 170, 234

Perfusionist, 20, 234

Personnel Director, 113

Pest Control Worker, 191

Pet Shop Manager, 191

Petroleum Engineer, 14, 50, 56, 98, 146

Petrologist, 95, 98, 234

Pharmacist, 23, 50, 53, 98, 164, 234

Pharmacologist, 50, 53, 143, 164, 235

Pharmacologist Sales Representative, 53

Photo-optics Technician, 80, 235

Photoengraver, 119, 235

Photogrammetrist, 56, 95, 98, 235

Photographer, 8, 29, 32-33, 59, 95, 155, 191

Photojournalist, 32

Physiatrist, 235

Physical Distribution Manager, 188

Physical Education Instructor, 173

Physical Therapist, 20, 41, 152, 235

Physical Therapy Assistant, 20

Physician (See various specialties)

Physician Assistant, 20, 23, 25, 143, 164

Physicist, 14, 17, 35, 53, 77, 98, 134, 161, 216, 231

Physiologist, 17, 41, 164, 173, 235

Pipefitter, 65, 235

Pipeline Engineer, 56, 146

Plant Breeder, 44, 110, 235

Plant Engineer, 116

Plant Geneticist, 92, 110

Plasterer, 65, 235-236

Plastic Surgeon, 143, 235

Plastics Engineer, 50, 116, 137, 146

Playwright, 83, 236

Plumber, 65, 204

Podiatric Assistant, 20

Podiatrist, 143, 236

Police Commissioner, 125, 236

Police Officer, 125, 170

Political Consultant, 167

Political Scientist, 104, 158, 167, 185

Politician, 167

Polygraph Examiner, 125, 215, 236

Preschool Teacher, 74

Priest, 176

Principal, 74

Printing Press Operator, 119

Prison Recreation Specialist, 173

Private Duty Nurse, 152

Private Investigator, 125

Process Engineer, 116

Proctologist, 236

Product Manager, 131

Production Manager, 86, 113

Professional Athlete, 173

Project Manager, 65

Proofreader, 59, 83, 89

Prosthetic and Orthotic Technician, 20

Psychiatric Nurse, 170

Psychiatrist, 143, 164, 170, 236

Psychologist, 74, 158, 170, 172, 182, 185, 236

Public Accountant, 11, 13

Public Administrator, 104, 158, 185

Public Health Educator, 102, 237

Public Health Service Officer, 102, 237

Public Health Statistician, 102

Public Information Specialist, 149

Public Librarian, 128

Public Recreation Director, 167

Public Relations Specialist, 47, 59, 102, 155, 170, 230, 237

Public Safety Captain, 125

Public Works Engineer, 56

Publisher, 59, 83, 158, 211, 222

Puppeteer, 155, 237

Purchasing Agent, 11, 86, 107, 113, 131, 237

Quality Control Engineer, 116

Quality Control Technician, 80

Rabbi, 176

Radar Technician, 80, 134

Radiation Therapy Technologist, 23, 237

Radio and Electrical Inspector, 80

Radio Engineer, 77

Radio Equipment Technician, 149

Radio Repairer, 80

Radiographer, 35, 237

Radiologic Health Specialist, 23

Radiologic Technologist, 20

Radiologist, 143, 232, 237

Rancher, 92

Range Manager, 44, 92, 191

Reading Specialist/Consultant, 83

Real Estate Agent, 71, 131

Receptionist, 179, 230

Records Manager, 179

Recreation Facility Manager, 173

Recreational Therapist, 152, 237

Recruiter, 149

Reference Librarian, 128

Registered Nurse, 152, 237

Registrar, 74, 237

Religious Brother, 176, 238

Religious Education Teacher, 176

Religious Sister, 176, 238

Reporter, 59, 83, 104, 167, 173, 179, 220

Reproductive Endocrinologist, 143

Research Analyst, 11, 71, 95, 104, 131, 134, 158, 170, 230, 238

Research Assistant, 8, 27, 41, 72, 95, 104, 117, 158-159, 167, 185

Research Associate, 26

Research Engineer, 14, 50, 56, 116, 137, 146

Research Technician, 35

Researcher, 107, 176

Resident Manager, 113

Resort Manager, 173

Respiratory Therapist, 41, 152, 164, 238

Respiratory Therapy Technician, 20

Restaurant Manager, 47, 86

Rigger, 65, 238

Robotics Technician, 62, 80

Roofer, 65

ROTC Instructor, 149

Safety Engineer, 14, 50, 56, 65, 77, 116, 137, 146, 238

Sales Manager, 47, 71, 107, 131

Sales Promotion Manager, 131

Sales Representative, 53, 71, 131, 230

Sales Supervisor, 131

Salesperson, 62, 72, 80, 131, 230, 239

Salvation Army Officer, 176

Sanitary Engineer, 56, 102, 146, 238

School Administrator, 47, 167

School Counselor, 182

School Nurse, 152

School Psychologist, 74, 172, 182

School Superintendent, 74, 238

Sculptor, 32

Secondary School Teacher, 74

Secretary, 83, 179, 203, 229-231

Securities Analyst, 71, 238

Securities Clerk, 38, 238

Securities Sales Agent, 131, 238

Security Officer, 125, 238

Seed Analyst, 44, 92, 110

Seismologist, 35, 95, 98, 161, 238

Service Station Worker, 188

Set Designer, 155

Sheet Metal Worker, 65, 239

Ship's Pilot, 149

Shoe Repairer, 119

Sign Painter, 32

Silviculturist, 44, 92, 110, 239

Singer, 155

Ski Instructor, 173

Smoke Jumper, 92

Social Service Aide, 107, 182

Social Service Director, 182

Social Service Worker, 125

Social Worker, 26, 74, 102, 107, 158, 170, 176, 182-185, 218, 226, 234, 236, 239

Sociologist, 26, 95, 182, 185, 187, 221, 226, 234, 239

Software Engineer, 62

Software Package Developer, 62

Software Salesperson, 62, 239

Soil Conservationist, 17, 44, 92, 95, 110, 239

Soil Scientist, 239

Sous Chef, 68, 239

Special Agent, 125, 224, 239

Special Collections Librarian, 128

Special Education Teacher, 74, 239

Speech Pathologist, 89, 170, 239

Speech Writer, 59, 83

Sports Marketer, 173, 239

Stage Manager, 155

Statistician, 11, 38, 62, 71, 102, 134-135, 217, 240

Stockbroker, 38, 71, 240

Stone Mason, 65, 240

Store Controller, 131

Store Manager, 47, 83, 131

Storeroom Supervisor, 86

Stratigrapher, 98, 240

Structural Engineer, 29, 56, 240

Surgeon, 92, 110, 143, 164, 235, 241

Surgical Technician, 20, 240

Surveying Technician, 167, 182, 185

Surveyor, 29, 92, 95, 98, 134, 235, 240

Systems Analyst, 11, 35, 38, 62, 116, 128, 134, 137, 149, 240

Systems Consultant, 62

Systems Engineer, 14, 116, 137, 146

Systems Manager, 62

Tailor, 107, 240

Tax Accountant, 11

Tax Attorney, 122

Tax Preparer, 11-12, 39, 71

Taxonomist, 41, 44, 92, 191, 240

Teacher, 5, 9, 74-76, 149, 155, 176, 215, 239, 241-242

Teacher Aide, 74

Teachers, 6-7, 210

Technical Assistant, 83

Technical Writer, 23, 26, 29, 53, 59, 62, 68, 71, 77, 80, 83, 89, 98, 104, 167, 182, 191, 241

Telephone Installer/Repairer, 140

Terrazzo Worker, 65, 241

Test Engineer, 137

Textile Engineer, 50

Therapist (See various specialties)

Tilesetter, 65

Time Study Engineer, 116

Tissue Technologist, 23, 241

Title Attorney, 122, 241

Tool and Die Maker, 119, 134

Topographic Engineer, 149

Traffic Court Magistrate, 122

Traffic Manager, 47, 188, 241

Train Conductor, 188

Trainer, 74, 149, 152, 173

Translator, 83, 89, 149

Transmissions Engineer, 77

Transportation Engineer, 56, 188

Travel Agent, 89

Treasurer, 11-12, 38-39, 72, 135

Tree Nursery Manager, 92

Tree Surgeon, 92, 110, 241

Truck Driver, 188, 228

Trust Administrator, 38, 71, 241

Tutor, 74-75, 171, 183, 241-242

TV Director, 32, 47, 59

TV Technician, 80

Typesetter, 242

Typist, 179

Underwriter, 11, 242

Upholsterer, 107, 119, 242

Urban Planner, 29, 56, 71, 95, 167, 185, 242

Urologist, 143, 164, 242

Vending Machine Servicer, 140

Veterinarian, 17, 41, 143, 164, 191, 193

Veterinary Assistant, 191

Veterinary Technician, 20

Virologist, 44, 92, 242

VISTA/Peace Corps Volunteer, 89

Vocational Rehabilitation Counselor, 74, 170, 182, 242

Warden, 125

Warehouse Manager, 47

Watchmaker, 140

Welder, 119, 242

Wholesaler, 47, 230, 242

Wildlife Biologist, 191

Wildlife Manager, 92

Wood Scientist, 53

Wood Technologist, 44, 92

X-ray Technician, 20, 237

YMCA/YWCA Director, 47, 113

Youth Minister, 176

Zookeeper, 191

Zoologist, 41, 191, 232